JESUS AND TRUE FATHER ARE ONE

Kerry K. Williams

Cover and graphic layout by Su-won Hadj-amar

'Jesus & True Father are One' logo by Yeonah Lee Moon

To 왕님 and Kook Jin nim.
Thank you for your incredible love
and loyalty to Father.

Acknowledgments

I would like to thank Su-won Hadj-amar and Rosemary Yokoi for their expert help preparing the book for print. Heartfelt gratitude goes to our Queen, Yeonah Moon. Without your support and encouragement this book would not have been written.

And, finally, thanks to my dear husband Douglas, for showing me Christ's love on a daily basis.

Table of Contents

INTRODUCTION

Understanding the oneness of Jesus and True Father is essential for Christians at this watershed moment in human history. The returning Jesus was born in 1920 in Jeong-Ju, in what is now North Korea. His parents converted to Christianity when Sun Myung Moon was ten years old. Korea was under Japanese occupation, and the young Moon witnessed tremendous suffering in the world around him. He became deeply religious, and often prayed to discern how a good God could allow so much human misery. Then, on Easter morning in 1935, Jesus of Nazareth appeared to fifteen-year-old Sun Myung Moon as he was praying in the Korean mountains. In a voice filled with sadness, Jesus directly appealed to the teenager to continue the work which had been left unfinished for nearly two thousand years. Jesus asked the Korean youth to complete the task of establishing God's Kingdom on earth. After initially refusing to accept such a difficult mission, Reverend Moon finally said yes. It was a decision that forever shifted his life trajectory:

> My encounter with Jesus changed my life. His sorrowful expression was etched into my heart as if it had

been branded there. I immersed myself completely in the Word of God. I experienced a series of days like these that led me into a deeper and deeper world of prayer. I embraced new words of truth that Jesus was giving me directly and let myself be completely captivated by God...[1]

During the nine years he discovered the contents of the *Divine Principle*,[2] Reverend Moon totally immersed himself in the study of the Bible. A school friend during that time said that in his room he kept three Bibles—one in Korean, one in English, and one in Japanese, which he studied continuously.

In the book of Revelation, Jesus confirms that it is he, himself, bearing a new name, who will return at the Second Advent:

> He who conquers, I will make him a pillar in the temple of my God; never shall he go out of it, and I will write on him the name of my God, and the name of the city of my God, the new Jerusalem which comes down from my God out of heaven, and my own new name.
> *Revelation 3:12*

Jesus of Nazareth and Sun Myung Moon are two individuals who lived two thousand years apart. Physically, they are separate entities who existed in different continents, cultures, and centuries. In essence, however, they are the same being with the same spirit. They are True Adam, the beloved Son whom God tragically lost as a result of the Fall. Because humankind died spiritually through the first man, God sent His Son again to restore our spiritual life *(1 Corinthians 15:22)*. We became separated from God and needed a relationship with someone who could bridge the chasm between us and the Father. We fell into spiritual depravity and required a Savior who could bring us back to our original position as children of God.

Christ exists in a different dimension, unlike any other person who has ever lived. Trying to understand the nature of Christ can be compared to a one dimensional line seeking to comprehend a two dimensional plane, or a two dimensional plane trying to figure out a three dimensional cube. Jesus alluded to his special origin in passages such as *John 6:38*, "For I have come down from heaven, not to do my own will but the will of Him who sent me."

The ontology of Christ is *sui generis*. Because of his unparalleled status, we cannot make judgments about him based on anyone else. Unlike us, Christ pre-existed within the Father:

> He is the image of the invisible God, the firstborn over all creation. For by him all things were created that are in heaven and that are on earth, visible and invisible, whether thrones or dominions or principalities or

powers. All things were created through him and for him. And he is before all things, and in him all things consist. *Colossians 1:15-17*

The Colossians passage indicates that the Son of God dwelled within God prior to the creation of the universe. Jesus declared his unique existence in the book of Revelation when he said, "I am the Alpha and the Omega, the First and the Last, the Beginning and the End." *(Revelation 22:13)*

In spite of strenuous efforts made by many scientists to divorce science from religion, modern science now posits that the universe, including the elements of time and space, must have had a beginning. The discovery of cosmic microwave background radiation by scientists Arnio Penzias and Robert Wilson in the 1960s inadvertently affirmed the opening chapters of Genesis.[3]

But science cannot tell us *who* created the temporal and spatial dimensions that exist within the physical world. Christians, however, not only name the *who* as "Heavenly Father"; we also believe that Jesus, His Son, has been eternally present within Him *(John 14:11)*.

Reverend Moon used the term "God of Night" in the later years of his ministry to describe the God who existed prior to the creation. This teaching, among his last revelations, was one of the final precious gifts that the returning Jesus saved for the right time to share. Less than two months before his death, Reverend Moon said, "Where I came from is different than where you come from. I am fundamentally different from you. After I found the secrets of heaven and earth, I have lived accordingly."[4] He was telling us that he, like Jesus of Nazareth, had come from, and would be returning to, the God of Night.[5]

Those who do not have a Christian background may struggle to comprehend the seemingly incomprehensible nature of someone who has always existed. This is where humility is needed. Unlike Christ, we are resultant, created beings, who exist within the confines of time and space. We are also sinners in need of salvation. Our intellect has limits and can only take us so far. We would do well to learn from the sincere heart of King David:

> You, God, are my God, earnestly I seek you,
> I thirst for you, my whole being longs for you,
> in a dry and parched land where there is no water.
> *Psalm 63:1*

It was the Messiah himself who revealed to us that his death on the cross was not God's primary will. True Father clarified that the crucifixion was God's secondary path of salvation. Because of his premature demise, Jesus was not able to share all that God wanted to say through him:

> There is so much more I want to tell you, but you cannot bear it now. When the spirit of truth comes, he will

guide you into all the truth. He will not speak on his
own but will tell you what he has heard. He will tell
you about the future. He will bring me glory by telling
you whatever he receives from me. *John 16:12-14*

Appearing again on earth after two thousand years, the
completed teachings of Christ have been recorded and released in the Eight Great Textbooks.[6] Just as Jesus fulfilled
the Old Testament prophecies through his life and teachings, so did Reverend Moon fulfill the promises of the New
Testament through his ninety-two years on earth.

The singular nature of God's lineage also points to the
oneness of the two men who came as True Adam. God,
our original Parent, wanted to live on the earth through
Adam, Eve, and their descendants *(Genesis 1:27-28)*. To believe in one God must imply that He will only have one lineage. The famous prayer of the Hebrews declares, "Hear,
O Israel: the Lord our God, the Lord is one." Jesus asked
believers to join him in becoming one with the Father:

I do not pray for these alone, but also for those who
will believe in me through their word; that they all may
be one, as You, Father, are in me, and I in you; that they
also may be one in us, that the world may believe that
You sent me. And the glory which You gave me I have
given them, that they may be one just as we are one: I
in them, and You in me; that they may be made perfect

in one, and that the world may know that You have
sent me, and have loved them as You have loved me.
John 17:20-23

In his 1974 speech at Madison Square Garden, Reverend Moon proclaimed, "There is only one God, one Christ, one Bible." In 2010, he handwrote a formal declaration, which included the following:

> The King of Kings is one being, God, and the True
> Parent is one person, one parent. The people of ten
> thousand generations are likewise the citizens of one
> lineage, and the children of one Heavenly Kingdom...[7]

Humankind is largely unaware of the tragic usurpation of lineage which occurred at the time of the Fall. Christ, the sole bearer of God's seed, has been tasked with the difficult job of "regrafting" us into the original lineage of God. When Jesus said, "I am the vine and you are the branches" *(John 15:5)*, he was indicating that only through him could we become one family under God.

While on earth, the returning Jesus, King of Kings *(Revelation 17:14, 19:16)*, established God's eternal presence on earth through the Three Kingships.[8] Sun Myung Moon, the First King of Cheon Il Guk,[9] no longer lives in his physical body, but he has not left us. His heir and successor, Hyung Jin Sean Moon, has taken the position of the Second King of Cheon Il Guk, and is continuing his Father's work. The Second King is not Christ himself; he is the *teshinja* (representative body) who bears the responsibility to continue Christ's lineage, as well as preserve his teachings and traditions. Through the inauguration of the Three Kingships, the messianic line of Jesus Christ and Sun Myung Moon will live eternally in the physical and spiritual realms.

Each of the chapters that follow, bound together by a common theme, are arranged in three sections. The first section tells a story or stories about Jesus and/or True Father[10] that illustrate the chapter theme, the second part contains my reflections, and the third section provides scriptural references.

Centering on the Holy Scriptures from the Old, New, and Completed Testaments,[11] I invite you to explore the beautiful unity of Jesus Christ and True Father.

They are the sons in whom our Heavenly Father delights, the unblemished lambs whose lives were complete offerings to Heaven.

CHAPTER 1

Christ exists as God's substantial body

The Ark brought to Jerusalem

Again David gathered all the choice men of Israel, thirty thousand. And David arose and went with all the people who were with him from Baale Judah to bring up from there the ark of God, whose name is called by the Name, the Lord of Hosts, who dwells between the cherubim. So they set the ark of God on a new cart, and brought it out of the house of Abinadab, which was on the hill; and Uzzah and Ahio, the sons of Abinadab, drove the new cart. And they brought it out of the house of Abinadab, which was on the hill, accompanying the ark of God; and Ahio went before the ark. Then David and all the house of Israel played music before the Lord on all kinds of instruments of fir wood, on harps, on stringed instruments, on tambourines, on sistrums, and on cymbals. *2 Samuel 6:1-5*

Whatever the Father does

So, because Jesus was doing these things on the Sabbath, the Jewish leaders began to persecute him. In his defense Jesus said to them, "My Father is always at His work to this very day, and I too am working." For this reason they tried all the more to kill him; not only was he breaking the Sabbath, but he was even calling God his own Father, making himself equal with God.

Jesus gave them this answer, "Very truly I tell you, the Son can do nothing by himself; he can do only what he sees his Father doing, because whatever the Father does the Son also does. For the Father loves the Son and shows him all He does. Yes, and He will show him even greater works than these, so that you will be amazed. For just as the Father raises the dead and gives them life, even so the Son gives life to whom he is pleased to give it. Moreover, the Father judges no one, but has entrusted all judgment to the Son, that all may honor the Son just as they honor the Father. Whoever does not honor the Son does not honor the Father, who sent him." *John 5:16-23*

Commentary

Christ is the key to understanding the Old as well as the New Testament. The more we study the Bible, the more we find it to be one story culminating in the person of Jesus. The Old Testament is filled with Christophanies[12] and foreshadowings of the Messiah to come. As the Alpha and Omega *(Revelation 22:13)*, Jesus presides in, as well as completes, all the stories and promises of the Hebrew Bible *(Hebrews 1:1-2)*.

Although King David was a deeply flawed individual, he can be viewed as a foreshadowing of Christ. David and Jesus were both born in Bethlehem. The shepherd boy grew up in humble circumstances, yet ascended to the throne of Israel. Jesus was born in obscure surroundings, and became the King of Kings. David was a shepherd; Christ was both the Good Shepherd and Shepherd King *(John 10:11, Psalm 23)*. David was a man who sought after God's heart *(1 Samuel 13:14)*; Jesus was the Son who did everything the Father asked of him *(John 14:31)*.

David demonstrated his humility to God and Christ-to-come when he travelled with thirty thousand of his finest soldiers to transfer the Ark of the Covenant from the home of Abinadab to Jerusalem. In doing so, David sought to revive the proper worship of the God of Israel, which had been in steady decline. The Ark of the Covenant can also be viewed as a prefiguring of Christ. Because Adam fell by uniting with Satan's false words, God's Logos could not take root in man. The tablets of stone symbolized the immutable Word of God which would later be manifested through the person of Jesus *(John 1:1)*. By restoring the Ark of the Covenant to a central position among the Israelites, David was presaging allegiance to Christ, the Word in human form.

Hundreds of messianic prophecies were fulfilled through the coming of Jesus, the man who was 100% God and 100% human. During his time on earth, he walked every step with God. Jesus was both the original "I am" *(John 8:58)* and the fruit of God's logos. The Jewish leaders condemned him for working on the Sabbath because they failed to recognize that it was God Himself who had chosen to heal the invalid on the day of rest. Jesus is the "express image" of the person of God *(Hebrews 1:3)*. Reverend Moon echoed this description of Christ when he said, "To resolve human suffering, God has sent a substantial incarnation as the master of ideals, justice and life. This is Jesus."[13]

As the body of God in the form of His Son, Reverend Moon was able to deeply empathize with the Father's heart:

> For fallen mankind, I am the savior. But from God's viewpoint, I am the True Son and True Parent who will fulfill the true love ideal of creation that was lost in the beginning. The savior is the one who pioneered the path of sacrifice, offering his life to relieve God's anguish that began with the Fall. The savior is not only living in glory. He weeps together with God's heart and is deeply concerned with bringing Satan to his knees.[14]

In the last several decades of his life, Reverend Moon shared more openly regarding his own incarnation: "When you go to the spirit world, I will be governing everything. It will not be me, however, but God. I am God's body."[15]

As the word made flesh, Christ is the strong and righteous father whose inner heart is more merciful than the most tender-hearted mother. He is the earthly vessel through whom God could take residence. The Messiah is proof that God has not abandoned us and will sacrifice that which is most precious in order to save us. His presence on the earth joined our humanity to His divinity. For all eternity, Jesus will be the way to the Father.

In his classic *Mere Christianity*, C.S. Lewis stated that Jesus could only be one of three things: Lunatic, Liar, or Lord:

> I am trying here to prevent anyone saying the really foolish thing that people often say about Him: I'm ready to accept Jesus as a great moral teacher, but I don't accept his claim to be God. That is the one thing we must not say. A man who was merely a man and said the sort of things Jesus said would not be a great moral teacher. He would either be a lunatic—on the level with the man who says he is a poached egg—or else he would be the Devil of Hell. You must make your choice. Either this man was, and is, the Son of God, or else a madman or something worse. You can shut him up for a fool, you can spit at him and kill him as a demon or you can fall at his feet and call him Lord and God, but let us not come with any patronising nonsense about his being a great human teacher. He has not left that open to us. He did not intend to... Now it seems to me obvious that He was neither a lunatic nor a fiend: and consequently, however strange or terrifying or unlikely it may seem, I have to accept the view that He was and is God.[16]

Scots preacher "Rabbi" John Duncan expressed the same sentiment: "Christ either deceived mankind by conscious fraud, or He was Himself deluded and self-deceived, or He was Divine. There is no getting out of this trilemma. It is inexorable."[17]

God, who is invisible, created both the physical and spiritual worlds. As our Creator, He is also our sovereign ruler. But how did He intend to have loving dominion over His creation? Heavenly Father desired to live on earth and in heaven through establishing His lineage on the physical plane, beginning with the body of Adam. Adam was born from the seed of God and was to have become God in the flesh. Reverend Moon explained:

> God wanted to enter and dwell in Adam to become the incorporeal Father, and He wanted Adam to become the corporeal father. Thus, Adam should have become God in the flesh. Why does God need a body of flesh? Because the incorporeal God cannot have dominion over the corporeal world that He created, God needs an incarnation of God.[18]

Due to the Fall, God lost the opportunity to dwell within His creation. Through the misuse of love, Adam was claimed by Satan as his descendant. As mentioned earlier, Jesus' presence on earth was symbolically manifested through the Ark of the Covenant, which contained the unchanging Word of God. Because Adam failed to become the Incarnation of the Word, God's Logos became separated from man. By uniting with the Word, i.e. the symbolic Christ, a foundation could be made to later receive Jesus, the Word made flesh. The ambulant Hebrew tribes, whose camp formation encircled the Tabernacle, prefigured the nation which was to have recognized and obeyed the Messiah as its center.

How precious is the person of Jesus, that God should work for four thousand years for one babe to be born in the city of Bethlehem? How valuable is the man Sun Myung Moon, that God should have persevered for two thousand years more so that His Son could be born in the province of Jeong-Ju?

As descendants of the Fall, we are in desperate need of the Word of God. After receiving Christ, we participate in our own recreation through actionizing Biblical truths, striving to live from the victory he has given us.

With Christ, however, the opposite is true. He was born from the seed of God, and grew into full maturity as God's Son *(Luke 2:52, Hebrews 5:7-9)*. The difference between Christ and us is that he alone became the complete substantiation of the Word of God. To study his life and teachings imparts Scripture because he *is* Scripture.

Scripture

For a child will be born to us, a son will be given to us; And the government will rest on his shoulders; And his name will be called Wonderful Counselor, Mighty God, Eternal Father, Prince of Peace. *Isaiah 9:6*

He said to them, "But who do you say that I am?" Simon Peter answered and said, "You are the Christ, the Son of the living God." *Matthew 16:15-16*

In the beginning was the Word, and the Word was with God, and the Word was God. He was in the beginning with God. All things were made through him, and without him nothing was made that was made. In him was life, and the life was the light of men. And the light shines in the darkness, and the darkness did not comprehend it. *John 1:1-5*

And the Word became flesh, and dwelt among us, and we beheld his glory, glory as of the only begotten from the Father, full of grace and truth. *John 1:14*

Jesus answered and said to them, "Destroy this temple, and in three days I will raise it up." Then the Jews said, "It has taken forty-six years to build this temple, and will you raise it up in three days?" But he was speaking of the temple of his body. *John 2:19-2*

Then Jesus, still teaching in the temple courts, cried out, "Yes, you know me, and you know where I am from. I am not here on my own, but He who sent me is true. You do not know Him, but I know Him because I am from Him and He sent me." *John 7:28-29*

Then they asked him, "Where is your father?" "You do not know me or my Father," Jesus replied. "If you knew me, you would know my Father also." *John 8:19*

"I and the Father are one." The Jews took up stones again to stone him. Jesus answered them, "I showed you many good works from the Father; for which of them are you stoning me?" The Jews answered him, "For a good work we do not stone you, but for blasphemy; and because you, being a man, make yourself out to be God." *John 10:30-33*

...yet for us there is but one God, the Father, from whom all things came and for whom we live; and there is but one Lord, Jesus Christ, through whom all things came and through whom we live. *1 Corinthians 8:6*

For by one Spirit we were all baptized into one body, whether Jews or Greeks, whether slaves or free, and we were all made to drink of one Spirit. *1 Corinthians 12:13*

For in him all the fullness of Deity dwells in bodily form. *Colossians 2:9*

There is one body and one Spirit, just as you were called in one hope of your calling; one Lord, one faith, one baptism; one God and Father of all, who is above all, and through all, and in you all. *Ephesians 4:4-6*

For this reason also, God highly exalted him, and bestowed on him the name which is above every name, so that at the name of Jesus every knee will bow, of those who are in heaven and on earth and under the earth, and that every tongue will confess that Jesus Christ is Lord, to the glory of God the Father. *Philippians 2:9-11*

...Jesus set the standard that God and he were one, not two. He had the mind-set that if God lives forever, he would also live forever. If God is unchanging, then he would also be unchanging. If God is infinitely merciful, then he would also be infinitely merciful. In other words, because he could feel and unite with the internal heart of God more than anyone else, Jesus could set the standard of victory during the conflict against Satan. *Sun Myung Moon 10/27/1957*

After being born on this earth, Jesus claimed, "I am the only begotten Son of God!" He made the decisive proclamation,

"No one comes to the Father but by me," meaning that in history up until his coming, no one could fully receive God's love. Thus, Jesus expounded the ultimate standard, the level that God longs to see us attain. Jesus was the only person who claimed this relationship with God. We read his words in John 14, "Believe that I am in the Father and the Father in me." Thus, he declared that he is one with God. *Sun Myung Moon 2/28/1972*

The Bible calls Jesus the "only begotten Son." What does this mean? God's love is absolute love. Jesus was the first person in history who could receive the total love of God and represent that love to humankind. Because God gave Jesus the title, "only begotten Son," he could become our Savior. Jesus taught that he is the true Son of God from the standpoint of love. Therefore, only by going through Jesus can we make a relationship of love [with God]. *Sun Myung Moon 6/15/1986*

Ideology can connect all people, but a substantial body can only be linked to one person. Therefore, there are many people of faith who say that they believe in the ideology, but there will not be many who claim they are embodiments of that ideology. What I am saying is that there is no person of faith who can say, "God's mind is my mind, my mind is His. His sorrow is my sorrow." Have you ever felt Heaven's heart of grief that has been bound until today, the heart so sorrowful it feels as if your bones are melting? You must realize that no matter where Jesus went, he spent thirty-odd years on the earth with such an intense mind that he was constantly on the verge of losing consciousness and fainting. *Sun Myung Moon 3/23/1958*

The Bible says that you should believe in Jesus, long for him and love him. This is because the incarnation is closer to corporeal human beings than is the invisible God. *Sun Myung Moon 8/30/1959*

When God's artery moved, Jesus' artery moved. The movement of love was automatic because their blood was connected. Such a world transcends logic as we know it. *Sun Myung Moon 7/12/1959*

Jesus came as the true father of humanity and the true son of God, yet he died on the cross. He probably came with the one determination which God had toward human beings for four thousand years. Every limb and organ of Jesus' body represented the ideal which Heaven had tried to realize through human beings for four thousand years. He was the true son God searched for with yearning. Therefore, Jesus' eyes represented the eyes of God for four thousand years. His ears represented the ears of God for four thousand years. His mouth represented the mouth of God for four thousand years. The same must have been true of

Jesus' feelings and body. He was the culmination of history and an historical incarnation. Hence, Jesus said, "I came to complete the law." The law's purpose was the same as his. *Sun Myung Moon 7/26/1959*

Only two years and eight months of Jesus' life was enough time to influence two thousand years of history. He was dressed in rags and looked little better than something discarded, but he digested the worldly cultural reality and the situations around him, and his thought influenced people to the depth of their hearts. When you think about it, you should realize that it was more than Jesus' doing; it was the work of God. The same is true with me. Families, grandfathers, siblings, and parents came before me, but I was set apart from them because God called me. I am different from you. *Sun Myung Moon 9/2/2011*

I am fundamentally different from you. Only the God of Night teaches me. *Sun Myung Moon 6/21/2011*

...my spirit self can discuss matters with the God of Night, which is why, through the absolute universe and absolute love, I can know about the secret, heavenly world of today and the liberated kingdom of heaven for humankind. *Sun Myung Moon 4/24/2011*

I was born of a different seed from yours. Therefore, I have lived a different life and have come thus far. *Sun Myung Moon 4/21/2012*

The God of Night sleeps holding me in His chest. When His chest becomes warm holding me, He falls asleep. *Sun Myung Moon 7/9/2012*

CHAPTER 2

Through Christ we are reborn into the lineage of God

Belonging to Christ

When she found out she was rape-conceived, Juda Myers was devastated. Juda had grown up thinking that the reason she had been placed up for adoption was because her mother had died giving birth. But as an adult, she returned to the agency that had originally placed her up for adoption, and discovered the truth--she was born as the result of her mother being brutally raped.

Although Juda had been raised to be a strong believer in Christ, the thought entered her mind to commit suicide. She walked out of the agency and returned to her car, crying uncontrollably. As she sat alone in the front seat, she heard demonic voices whispering in her ear, "See, I told you you were worthless. I told you God had nothing to do with you."

She could actually feel demons running through her veins, pulsating like she'd never felt before. This was a new, totally alien experience for her; she heard the devil say, "All you have to do is cut your wrists and let all that nasty rapist blood flow out, nobody will care." She could feel that Satan was waiting for her at the other end. But then the voice of God entered her: "No! I have made you for a purpose!" And then, unexpectedly, Jesus was sitting next to her. She knew that he had come to save her. Out of her mouth she heard herself speak the words, "I can't do that because I belong to Christ." Right at that moment all the voices left; the pulsating in her veins ceased. She then heard the voice of God clearly say to her, "I placed you in the camp of the enemy to glorify My name."

On the following day, Juda's life was transformed when someone who knew nothing of her story, told her, "I know that God knew you before you were ever conceived." At that moment Juda knew that God Himself had a reason for her life. And that she belonged to Him.[19]

Commentary

How many of us have heard a similar voice to the one that Juda Myers heard in the front seat of her car? We may not have dealt with the same traumatic reality, but haven't some of us struggled with feelings of worthlessness before God?

In this "enlightened" age, the thought of original sin may seem passé, but the fractured state of the human psyche continues to be a stubborn universal reality. Is living in a broken world what God intended? Both Jesus and True Father spoke bluntly about the fact that at the start of the human race, something went terribly wrong.

The beginning point of accepting Christ as our Lord and Savior is the realization we are sinners. We admit our radical need for Christ and plead for forgiveness. We seek from him what we could never obtain on our own.

After being forgiven, however, we easily slip back into sinful, selfish thinking, and believe it is our natural state of existence. We relish the chance to point out the speck in our brother's eye without noticing the log firmly lodged in our own. Without the help of the Holy Spirit, it is impossible to realize that we were born from the love, life, and lineage of Satan. Science fiction abounds with stories of people being invaded and possessed by alien spirits and demons, but most of us are reluctant to consider the possibility that we could actually have descended from a lineage tainted by real evil.

Jesus states in *Matthew 23:33* that we are descendants of the serpent, a "brood of vipers." He declares in *John 8:44* that our paternal line originates from the adversary, Satan. In these passages, Jesus teaches us that human beings are born inheriting the flesh and blood of the original adulterer, the fallen archangel Lucifer. It was the returning Jesus, True Father, who exposed the devil's long-held secret that the Fall of Man was an act of illicit seduction. In the course of discovering the contents of the Bible-based Divine Principle, Reverend Moon received direct confirmation of this primordial tragedy from both God and Satan.[20]

Christ can declare his father is different than ours because he bears no trace of sin. It is the Messiah who both diagnoses our spiritual sickness and offers us the cure. Through cultivating a relationship with the wholly good son, we are able to renew our bond with the wholly good Father. The vicissitudes of life challenge our faith, but as we declare our insufficiency and our need for Christ, we come closer to God. The consistent need to return to him serves as a humble reminder of our frailty.

Christianity differs from other religions in its simplicity. The focus is not on a set of beliefs, sacraments, or ceremonies. Christ himself is the focal point. The peace we long for is found in the person of Jesus. We begin to receive Christ's peace when we recognize that sin creates a barrier between us and God that we cannot penetrate. When we wholeheartedly give ourselves to Jesus, he is able to provide the reconciliation with the Father that we all desire.

It was the presence of Jesus sitting next to Juda Myers that gave her the power to overcome thoughts of despair and suicide. Through his unconditional love, she could break free from destructive forces and draw near to God.

Like Nicodemus, we hear the voice of Christ telling us that we must be born again into the lineage of him who has no sin. We are triumphant over the devil because we are of Christ's bloodline. We know to whom we belong.

Scripture

Then the Lord saw that the wickedness of man was great on the earth, and that every intent of the thoughts of his heart was only evil continually. And the Lord was sorry that He had made man on the earth, and He was grieved in His heart. *Genesis 6:5-6*

Have mercy on me, O God,according to Your unfailing love;
according to Your great compassion
blot out my transgressions.
Wash away all my iniquity
and cleanse me from my sin.
For I know my transgressions,
and my sin is always before me.
Against You, You only, have I sinned
and done what is evil in Your sight,
so that You are proved right when You speak
and justified when You judge.
Surely I was sinful at birth,
sinful from the time my mother conceived me.
Surely You desire truth in the inner parts;
You teach me wisdom in the inmost place.
Cleanse me with hyssop, and I will be clean;
wash me, and I will be whiter than snow.
Let me hear joy and gladness;
let the bones You have crushed rejoice.

Hide Your face from my sins
and blot out all my iniquity.
Create in me a pure heart, O God,
and renew a steadfast spirit within me.
Do not cast me from Your presence
or take Your Holy Spirit from me.
Restore to me the joy of Your salvation
and grant me a willing spirit, to sustain me.
Then I will teach transgressors Your ways,
and sinners will turn back to You.
Save me from bloodguilt, O God,
the God who saves me,
and my tongue will sing of Your righteousness.
O Lord, open my lips,
and my mouth will declare Your praise.
You do not delight in sacrifice, or I would bring it;
You do not take pleasure in burnt offerings.
The sacrifices of God are a broken spirit;
a broken and contrite heart,
O God, You will not despise.
In Your good pleasure make Zion prosper;
build up the walls of Jerusalem.
Then there will be righteous sacrifices,
whole burnt offerings to delight You;
then bulls will be offered on Your altar. *Psalm 51:1-19*

Indeed, there is not a righteous man on earth who continually does good and who never sins. *Ecclesiastes 7:20*

The heart is deceitful above all things, And desperately wicked; Who can know it? *Jeremiah 17:9*

You snakes! You brood of vipers! How will you escape being condemned to hell? *Matthew 23:33*

You belong to your father, the devil, and you want to carry out your father's desires. He was a murderer from the beginning, not holding to the truth, for there is no truth in him. When he lies, he speaks his native language, for he is a liar and the father of lies. *John 8:44*

But to all who believed him and accepted him, he gave the right to become children of God. *John 1:12*

Now there was a Pharisee, a man named Nicodemus who was a member of the Jewish ruling council. He came to Jesus at night and said, "Rabbi, we know that you are a teacher who has come from God. For no one could perform the signs you are doing if God were not with him." Jesus replied, "Very truly I tell you, no one can see the kingdom of God unless they are born again." "How can someone be born when they are old?" Nicodemus asked. "Surely they cannot enter a second time into their mother's womb to be born!" Jesus answered, "Very truly I tell you, no one can enter the kingdom of God unless they are born of water and the Spirit. Flesh gives birth to flesh, but the Spirit gives birth to spirit. You should not be surprised at my saying, 'You must be born again.' " *John 3:1-7*

Jesus said to them, "Very truly I tell you, unless you eat the flesh of the Son of Man and drink his blood, you cannot have eternal life within you. But anyone who eats my flesh and drinks my blood has eternal life, and I will raise that person at the last day. For my flesh is true food, and my blood is true drink. Anyone who eats my flesh and drinks my blood remains in me, and I in him." *John 6:53-56*

I am the true vine, and my Father is the vinedresser. Every branch in me that does not bear fruit He takes away; and every branch that bears fruit He prunes, that it may bear more fruit. You are already clean because of the word which I have spoken to you. Abide in me, and I in you. As the branch cannot bear fruit of itself, unless it abides in the vine, neither can you, unless you abide in me. I am the vine, you are the branches. He who abides in me, and I in him, bears much fruit; for without me you can do nothing. If anyone does not abide in me, he is cast out as a branch and is withered; and they gather them and throw them into the fire, and they are burned. If you abide in me, and my words abide in you, you will ask what you desire, and it shall be done for you. *John 15:1-7*

For all who are being led by the Spirit of God, these are sons of God. *Romans 8:14*

Not only so, but we ourselves, who have the first fruits of the Spirit, groan inwardly as we wait eagerly for our adoption to sonship, the redemption of our bodies. *Romans 8:23*

So in Christ Jesus you are all children of God through faith. *Galatians 3:26*

And you He made alive, who were dead in trespasses and sins, in which you once walked according to the course of this world, according to the prince of the power of the air, the spirit who now works in the sons of disobedience, among whom also we all once conducted ourselves in the lusts of our flesh, fulfilling the desires of the flesh and of the mind, and were by nature children of wrath, just as the others. But God, who is rich in mercy, because of His great love with which He loved us, even when we were dead in trespasses, made us alive together with Christ (by grace you have been saved), and raised us up together, and made us sit together in the heavenly places in Christ Jesus, that in the ages to come He might show the exceeding riches of His grace in His kindness toward us in Christ Jesus. *Ephesians 2:1-7*

He who sins is of the devil, for the devil has sinned from the beginning. For this purpose the Son of God was manifested, that He might destroy the works of the devil. Whoever has been born of God does not sin, for His seed remains in him; and he cannot sin, because he has been born of God. *1 John 3:8-9*

And this is the testimony: that God has given us eternal life, and this life is in His Son. He who has the Son has life; he who does not have the Son of God does not have life. *1 John 5:11-12*

I, Jesus, have sent my angel to testify to you these things for the churches I am the root and the descendant of David, the bright morning star. *Revelation 22:16*

You know that the one who came to the earth on behalf of all people as the true person, the one of the heavenly lineage who had the original nature of creation, was none other than Jesus. *Sun Myung Moon 3/23/1958*

Why do we await the coming Lord? Why does humanity in Heaven and on earth await the day of Jesus' return? No matter how great one may be, everyone is at most an adopted son of God. Christ is to return with the mission of establishing the relationship of the heart with which people can become God's direct children. *Sun Myung Moon 7/26/1959*

Our real father is God, but Satan usurped the father's role. Therefore, Jesus said, "You are of your father the devil, and your will is to do your father's desires." Knowing the deplorable fact that you carry Satan's blood, out of shame you should have the courage to put yourself through trials to rid yourself of that stained, false blood. Have you ever thought of doing so? If you are someone who strikes your body with fury saying "You lump of flesh" you are a loyal citizen of heaven. *Sun Myung Moon 10/29/1961*

The Messiah may be able to remove the satanic blood, but you must obey and follow him so that he can do that. *Sun Myung Moon 10/13/1970*

How many people have faith to the extent that they actually want to go into the flesh and body of Jesus? You cannot enter the body of Jesus except through heart and love. Only love can connect us with Jesus, not the truth nor righteousness. Before life there is love. Man is born through parental love. Without that love there is nothing that can connect us to God, but with love it is completely possible. Love goes beyond history, transcending time and space. *Sun Myung Moon 10/13/1970*

The human fall was caused by someone else staining the blood or the blood lineage of man through the fallen act. So, unless we can restore or shift the blood lineage into the original status, we cannot work the providence of restoration through man. God had to wait so long, through more than 6,000 years of sinful human history because He wanted to commence His providence of restoration by finding one man having nothing to do with stained love. *Sun Myung Moon 1/18/1973*

Since humankind has received satanic blood, people cannot return to God on their own. So the Messiah must accomplish absolute restoration of the lineage, renewing the blood line that was defiled by Satan. This transition must be made. This is why the Messiah must surely come. Without his coming, there will be no restoration of lineage. *Sun Myung Moon 1/7/1988*

In order to enter the Kingdom of heaven, the world has to go in one line through the one blood lineage. *Sun Myung Moon 1/2/1997*

Adam's family bore Satan's blood lineage... God could not say that the problem was the fallen blood lineage, which has to be cut off because the Fall took place in the realm of incompleteness centered on illicit love. The same is true with Satan. In the future, these things should become known. After Adam and Eve learned the truth, Adam's family and tribe had to know it. However, because of the Fall, there were no such tribes. Satan cannot teach this

truth either. Who has to teach it? In the providence of restoration, the Messiah has to come and replace the false
life and false blood lineage. *Sun Myung Moon 1/2/1997*

....

People in today's world boast of their social status or
family background, all the while unaware that they were
misbegotten at birth. They do not know that they were
born from the love, life, and lineage of Satan, the enemy
of God. This is a serious problem. Due to the human Fall,
all people have been born from Satan's love. Satan's love
has been passed down through the generations to their
parents and then to them. Satan's blood is flowing in the
life of every mother and in the life of every father, and
that blood now flows in each of us. Each of us is a fruit
of these three. For this reason, each of you belongs to the
lineage of Satan. To put it another way, Satan's blood is
running through your veins... Meanwhile, God strives
to redeem those same men and women and transform
them into the pure and wholesome men and women of
His original vision. Your beginning was in Satan's love.
You were born from his lineage. Your starting-point was
wrong. Since you came from the wrong starting-point,
you must return to the correct starting-point. Where is
that correct starting-point? How far back do we need
to go? We need to go back to the origin. As we originated from false parents, we need to return and start anew
from true parents. How serious is this? It is imperative to

inherit God's love, life and lineage afresh. *True Family: Gateway to Heaven, pp. 84-85*

Because Jesus was born on the foundation of a purified lineage, having nothing to do with Satan, he is indeed the Son of God. He could finally claim, "I am the only begotten Son of God." No one like Jesus had ever appeared before in human history... There have been other religious founders and saviors in history, but none of them was born relating to God as a son to his Parent, because they did not have a purified lineage, unstained by Satan's polluted blood. Neither Buddha nor Confucius nor Mohammed came from such a background. Therefore, Jesus' birth on earth was truly the hope of all humankind. It is through the glory of his person that we can receive new life and resurrection. *Sun Myung Moon 2/21/1972*

Jesus said, "Repent." But how can we repent? Jesus meant repent for having false lineage and misuse of sexual organ. Fallen Adam and Eve, do you think God would want to get close to them? In the Bible it says, "Love your enemy." But what is your enemy? It is your sexual organ and lineage. You gracious lady sitting in the front, your lineage is so filthy. You need a transfusion. Religions are prepared in history to receive the Lord. The Lord comes to clean the lineage. All human beings have Satan's blood - false lineage. Messiah comes as a doctor with all skills needed to change lineage and engraft to the True Olive Tree. From the Wild Olive Tree a thousand years old, we need only one bud. Is there a difference between the true bud and the false bud? A novice cannot tell. This is why religions have been chased out and persecuted. Do you have true lineage? Do you own true lineage? What kind do you have? Muddy, mixed, filthy? Does God expect such in the Kingdom of Heaven? *Sun Myung Moon 2/18/2001*

True Father, who carries the seed and DNA of life he received from his Father, who has no connection whatsoever to the fallen lineage, is the center. *Sun Myung Moon 8/30/2009*

One must resemble their parents on the base of being connected to the parents' tradition through blood lineage...When one is connected to their parents through a blood lineage, do they resemble their parents or not? If they want to have the same tradition as their parents, they must have the same blood lineage, and if they have the same tradition and blood lineage, they can resemble their parents. One tradition must have one blood lineage. *Sun Myung Moon 7/22/2012*

Who is supposed to carry out the conversion of the lineage? It cannot be performed by just anyone. You must know that in order to become the one that can perform it,

I walked the tearful path of the cross...It took thousands of years of hard work on God's part and my substantial life course, which was filled with hardships and suffering, to establish the victorious realm of the conversion of lineage. *Cheon Seong Gyeong,[21] p. 1271*

CHAPTER 3

Christ is the person who most deeply understands God's heart

Gethsemane

Then Jesus came with them to a place called Gethsemane, and said to the disciples, "Sit here while I go and pray over there." And he took with him Peter and the two sons of Zebedee, and he began to be sorrowful and deeply distressed. Then he said to them, "My soul is exceedingly sorrowful, even to death. Stay here and watch with me."

He went a little farther and fell on His face, and prayed, saying, "O My Father, if it is possible, let this cup pass from me; nevertheless, not as I will, but as You will."

Then he came to the disciples and found them sleeping, and said to Peter, "What! Could you not watch with me one hour? Watch and pray, lest you enter into temptation. The spirit indeed is willing, but the flesh is weak."

Again, a second time, he went away and prayed, saying, "O My Father, if this cup cannot pass away from me unless I drink it, Your will be done." And he came and found them asleep again, for their eyes were heavy.

So he left them, went away again, and prayed the third

time, saying the same words. Then he came to his disciples and said to them, "Are you still sleeping and resting? Behold, the hour is at hand, and the Son of Man is being betrayed into the hands of sinners. Rise, let us be going. See, my betrayer is at hand." *Matthew 26:36-46*

No one prayed like True Father

The morning rain persisted as I prayed inside the sanctuary of the Korean Presbyterian Church. The date was May 10, 1952. A fervent Christian, I spent nearly all my time witnessing, boasting about Jesus and introducing him to people. Whenever I met someone I told them I was a believer in Jesus, because I was in love with my Savior. I lived to bring lost souls to Jesus.

As I spoke to God that morning, I was internally preparing to meet the strange young man I had heard about--a preacher who was living in a tiny house in Pusan. One day a lady had come to my church and told me of this evangelist who had unusual beliefs. Somehow 1 became quite interested in her story. I set a one-week prayer condition, asking Heavenly Father, if it was His will, to help me go there and meet this young man. I thought, "If he is smart, and a person who can be used by God, I will lead him to the church and help him become a worker for the Lord." On this rainy day in May I had the inspiration to go. My motivation was quite clear. If this man was misguided in his efforts, I had to point him in the right direction.

The instructions I had been given to his home were vague, but after a long search I finally located a hut built of mud and stone. I walked inside and saw water leaking through a stained ceiling. The inside walls were made from soil; the earthen floor was covered with pieces of black plastic bags. It looked like a stable in the country-side. I noticed a round table on one side of the room with a box full of pencils on top. As I stared at the shabby room, I thought of how miserable someone would be if they had to spend their whole life in such a house.

Just then, a young man walked in. My first impression was that he looked like a factory worker. He was wearing a khaki hanbok (Korean traditional clothes), and an old brown jack-et. That young man was True Father. He asked me, "Where are you from?" After I explained, Father said, "Today is May 10. You came on a very meaningful day. After I escaped from North to South Korea, I began writing a precious book in this house. And today is the day that I finished writing it."

He continued, "I have just come back from the moun-tain where I prayed, 'God, You promised me that many people will gather under this precious Principle teaching. You promised me that You would build one world of love with these people who will come. But I haven't found a single person yet. God, please send me people. Especially send me the saints who believe in Jesus.'"

Then Father looked at me and said, "For the past sev-en years, God has been giving you so much love." I was amazed! How did he know that it had been exactly seven years earlier since I had dedicated my whole life to God?

Then Father began to teach me the Principle with much energy and enthusiasm, as if he were addressing thousands of people. I wondered why he was talking so forcefully, when it was only myself in front of him. The room was just large enough for two people; I was leaning away from him against the wall. His eyes were shining brilliantly as he taught me for over three hours.

After he finally finished, I thought, "That's enough for today." I started to leave the house, but he asked me, "It's not very special, but why don't we have dinner together?" Ignoring my protests, he insisted that I stay. Dinner was served on a tiny pine table, just big enough for one person. There was no rice, just barley, the badly-hulled type the government gave to refugees. He also served old, sour kimchee, and bean curd. Father asked me to pray for the meal, but I couldn't. Father had spoken so forcefully that I couldn't collect my thoughts; I had lost my nerve to say anything. After refusing his requests, he began to pray, "Heavenly Father, I want to fulfill Your will. I would like to solve Your grief. I would like to console You. You have been longing to find someone who can fulfill Your will. I want to fulfill Your will and restore the whole world. I will do everything for You. I have walked this far to achieve Your will, and I know that You have labored more than I have. I will fulfill Your will. I certainly will resolve all the sorrows that remain in You. I will find and establish Your nation and Your world on this earth. Look at me and be consoled, for I will be the one who comforts and pleases God."

All his words centered on consoling God. Crying as he prayed, his voice became choked with tears. He took a short rest and then resumed his prayer. It was a supplication that came out from his flesh and bone, from deep within his heart.

I had been praying for many hours every day, but it was always to petition God for the president of the country, for leaders of North and South Korea, for poor and unhappy people. I was also praying for more than one hundred members of my congregation by name. I would pray, "Oh, God, please give me this, help me in that, give me what I need."

But this young pastor only cared about relieving God's pain and suffering which extended to the entire world. Father told me, "Even though this room is shabby and unpresentable, I am opening a door for all mankind. I know that so many people have lost their way and don't know what to do. So many people are suffering. We have to help them. So l keep my door open twenty-four hours a day. The time will come when not only Christianity, but all the religions of the world can be unified."

I was deeply moved by his incredible sincerity and compassion towards his Heavenly Father. In all my life, I had never heard such a prayer.[22]

True Mother Hyun Shil Kang, First Queen of Cheon Il Guk

Commentary

1 Corinthians 2:11 tells us that our spirit within us knows our thoughts. So too, no one knows the thoughts and heart of God except the spirit of God. Christ, born of God's very seed, is fully imbued with the spirit of the Father, and knows His heart most completely.

Why, in Gethsemane, did our Savior cry out to be spared the cup of death? Was he demonstrating human weakness, as some have thought? In that case, one could argue that eighteenth-century American patriot Nathan Hale, before being hanged by the British as a spy, showed greater courage than Jesus in the Garden of Gethsemane. After having been summoned to the gallows, Hale stated, "I only regret that I have but one life to lose for my country."

Jesus asked not to die in the Garden because he knew the agonized heart of the Father. As the only begotten son, Jesus had the opportunity to end the historical loneliness of God by establishing His lineage on the earth. He knew that if he went the way of the cross, Heavenly Father would have to witness His beloved Son die a horribly cruel death. God would then have to painstakingly lay another foundation to send His Son again to the earth. Jesus asked the cup to be spared only thinking of the terrible suffering his Father would have to endure.

Jesus spent every moment of his life testifying to the heart and will of God. There was no moment that he lived for his own sake. He was keenly aware that God had spent four thousand years in preparation for him to be born. He knew that humanity could only be saved through being engrafted into the lineage of the Son of God.

Reverend Moon explained:

> Jesus was someone governed only by God. He consulted with God alone. He was the one who understood the internal love and heart of God most clearly. What situation does the Fall of humankind refer to? The Fall was not understanding the situation of God. The Fall was not understanding the heart of God. Therefore, God has been searching for the one individual who can be connected to His situation. He has been exerting Himself to search for the individual who can connect to His heart...[23]

> Because the mind of God and the mind of Jesus could become one incarnation in the actual world of substance, God could forge a direct relationship with Jesus. Because Jesus could possess the same heart and enter the same situation as God on behalf of the earth, the works of God could have been performed directly centering on human beings.[24]

The heart of Jesus was a sorrowful heart, because he knew the woeful situation of his Father. Jesus was the first person who truly understood God's inexpressible grief as a result of losing His children to Satan at the time of the Fall. As God's most faithful Son, Jesus clung to the will of Heaven in all circumstances. Although his hope was to continue serving God on earth, Jesus was ready to unite with whatever direction his Father needed him to take.

On the day that Hyun Shil Kang journeyed to Pusan to visit the "strange young man," True Father was immersed in prayer, beseeching God to send him the righteous Christians prepared to meet the returning Lord. True Mother Kang did not know then that Reverend Moon had narrowly escaped death in a North Korean prison camp and walked hundreds of miles south to begin rebuilding his ministry from a humble mud hut. Like Jesus, True Father never dwelled on his own difficult circumstances. The Presbyterian missionary was stunned by the tender, tearful prayer of the unusual preacher who only wanted to comfort God.

True Mother Kang was a woman of profound faith. But on May 10, 1952, she met someone whose bond with Heavenly Father was stronger and deeper than her own. The intense urgency of the young preacher's heart towards Heaven convicted her that the spirit of Jesus was indeed upon this man of God.

Scripture

Thus says the Lord: "Let not the wise man boast in his wisdom, let not the mighty man boast in his might, let not the rich man boast in his riches, but let him who boasts boast in this, that he understands and knows Me, that I am the Lord who practices steadfast love, justice, and righteousness in the earth. For in these things I delight, declares the Lord." *Jeremiah 9:23-24*

The Lord said to him, "Go, marry a promiscuous woman and have children with her, for like an adulterous wife this land is guilty of unfaithfulness to the Lord." *Hosea 1:2*

Yet I will show love to Judah; and I will save them—not by bow, sword or battle, or by horses and horsemen, but I, the Lord their God, will save them. *Hosea 1:7*

Then the Lord said to me, "Go again, love a woman who is loved by a lover and is committing adultery, just like the love of the Lord for the children of Israel, who look to other gods and love the raisin cakes of the pagans."
So I bought her for myself for fifteen shekels of silver, and one and one-half homers of barley. And I said to her, "You shall stay with me many days; you shall not play the harlot, nor shall you have a man —so, too, will I be toward you."
For the children of Israel shall abide many days without king or prince, without sacrifice or sacred pillar, without ephod or teraphim. Afterward the children of Israel shall return and seek the Lord their God and David their king. They shall fear the Lord and His goodness in the latter days. *Hosea 3:1-5*

All things have been handed over to me by my Father; and no one knows the Son except the Father; nor does anyone know the Father except the Son, and anyone to whom the Son wills to reveal Him. *Matthew 11:27*

Then he said: "A certain man had two sons. And the younger of them said to his father, 'Father, give me the portion of goods that falls to me.' So he divided to them his livelihood. And not many days after, the younger son gathered all together, journeyed to a far country, and there wasted his possessions with prodigal living. But when he had spent all, there arose a severe famine in that land, and he began to be in want. Then he went and joined himself to a citizen of that country, and he sent him into his fields to feed swine. And he would gladly have filled his stomach with the pods that the swine ate, and no one gave him anything.

But when he came to himself, he said, 'How many of my father's hired servants have bread enough and to spare, and I perish with hunger! I will arise and go to my father, and will say to him, "Father, I have sinned against heaven and before you, and I am no longer worthy to be called your son. Make me like one of your hired servants."'

And he arose and came to his father. But when he was still a great way off, his father saw him and had compassion, and ran and fell on his neck and kissed him. And the son said to him, 'Father, I have sinned against heaven and in your sight, and am no longer worthy to be called your son.' But the father said to his servants, 'Bring out the best robe and put it on him, and put a ring on his hand and sandals on his feet. And bring the fatted calf here and kill it, and let us eat and be merry; for this my son was dead and is alive again; he was lost and is found.' And they began to be merry.

Now his older son was in the field. And as he came and drew near to the house, he heard music and dancing. So he called one of the servants and asked what these things meant. And he said to him, 'Your brother has come, and because he has received him safe and sound, your father has killed the fatted calf.'

But he was angry and would not go in. Therefore his father came out and pleaded with him. So he answered and said to his father, 'Lo, these many years I have been serving you; I never transgressed your commandment at any time; and yet you never gave me a young goat, that I might make merry with my friends. But as soon as this son of yours came, who has devoured your livelihood with harlots, you killed the fatted calf for him.'

And he said to him, 'Son, you are always with me, and all that I have is yours. It was right that we should make merry and be glad, for your brother was dead and is alive again, and was lost and is found.' " *Luke 15:11-32*

I know Him, because I am from Him, and He sent me.
John 7:29

Jesus answered, "If I honor myself, my honor is nothing. It is my Father who honors me, of whom you say that He is your God. Yet you have not known Him, but I know Him. And if I say, 'I do not know Him,' I shall be a liar like you; but I do know Him and keep His word." *John 8:54-55*

I am the good shepherd; and I know my sheep, and am known by my own. As the Father knows me, even so I know the Father; and I lay down my life for the sheep. And other sheep I have which are not of this fold; them also I must bring, and they will hear my voice; and there will be one flock and one shepherd. *John 10:14-16*

I am the way and the truth and the life. No one comes to the Father except through me. If you really know me, you will know my Father as well. From now on, you do know Him and have seen Him. *John 14:6-7*

O righteous Father! The world has not known You, but I have known You; and these have known that You sent me. And I have declared to them Your name, and will declare it, that the love with which You loved me may be in them, and I in them. *John 17:25-26*

For the Spirit searches everything, even the depths of God. For who knows a person's thoughts except the spirit of that person, which is him? So, also no one comprehends the thoughts of God except the Spirit of God. Now we have received not the spirit of the world, but the Spirit who is from God, that we might understand the things freely given us by God. *1 Corinthians 2:1-12*

The body of Jesus Christ knew how to feel and experience God's shimjung,[25] and Jesus' heart knew how to feel God's shimjung. Therefore, Jesus' leaping heart, by adopting Heaven as the artery and humans as the vein, should have formed all relations whereby Jesus moves when Heaven moves and Jesus gets emotions when humans get emotions. That was the mission of Jesus Christ who came to this earth. However, there was no one who could understand the internal shimjung of Jesus Christ who felt God's shimjung, who could understand the external heart of Jesus who felt God's shimjung. For this reason, the heart of Jesus Christ was a heart that had experienced loneliness of which no one knew for thirty years of preparation period. Why did Jesus feel such sorrow? The reason is that, due to the fall of the human ancestors Adam and Eve, the will of God, who wished to enjoy glory through the attainment of the ideology of creation, did not become realized and all created things came to stand in a position of having lost their master. God who was looking at this came to feel inexpressibly lonely. Because Jesus knew of God's shimjung, Jesus also felt loneliness. Accordingly, you too should become the people who feel that the world of creation has become a world that is indescribably desolate like Jesus did. What kind of life did Jesus, who had passed through the thirty-year preparation period, live after that? When he came to appear upholding the will for God and preach the new Gospel before the Israelite people, whom God chose and raised after having toiled for four thousand years, his heart must have been overflowing with the indescribable sense of mission. You should not forget the fact that Jesus who, after liquidating the sorrowful life of thirty years by eliminating Heaven's sorrow and grief, bore the mission to restore again the hero of the lost Eden, appeared with a pulsating heart that was expressible to none...

Jesus' shimjung, who was looking over the distrusting Israelite people, might have been limitlessly sad. His sense of indignation might have been great, too. He might have felt eagerly like giving orders to judge them, making appeals and curses before Heaven. However, casting off such shimjung in entirety, pressing down the throbbing chest and pulsating heart, Jesus endured and forbore, thinking of the shimjung that God might have felt after Adam and Eve fell from Eden long ago, and harbored a sorrowful shimjung. Furthermore, you must understand that Jesus had placed his hope in the Israelite people who were putting up opposition...

Jesus' shimjung said, "Foxes have holes, and birds of the air have nests; but the son of man has nowhere to lay his head." *(Matthew 8:20)* You should be able to feel and experience the pulsating heart of Jesus who had to carry out the fight, clinging onto the will of Heaven in lonely circumstances this hour. The more he came to know of the huge effort God had made, the bigger the feeling of fretfulness and indignation must have been. The greater the hope and expectation of the chosen Israel, the more serious the cutting pain, pierced with bitter resentment, in the heart of Jesus Christ must have been. You must feel the state in which Jesus' heart might have been when he stepped out of the house, without uttering a word, bearing all this. You must understand that this is the very time when you must reflect, in a manner of awareness, to find out in what state is your heart pulsating today...

Jesus went out to the wilderness, leaving behind the people of the nation and fasted for forty days. As Jesus thought about having to go out into the wilderness and wander around in solitude without being able to eat anything in this manner, he could have felt terribly mortified. However, having thought of God's shimjung that had endured and forborne for four thousand years, Jesus who still felt some lingering expectation toward this people of the nation made the sacrificial offering on the people's level before God for forty days without eating anything in the wilderness to establish the foundation of the second life for these people. This you should be aware of.

You may know too, from your experience of fasting, that Jesus grew gaunt and his body wasted with hunger during the forty day fast. Although Jesus felt his shimjung indescribably squeezed and his heart became weak during the forty-day fasting course, it was because he felt God's shimjung deep in his heart that he crossed the hill of the forty-day fast. What then can we do today? We must become friends of Jesus' who can understand his situation and do something about it. At the same time, we must become friends who, holding onto Jesus Christ who could not eat, can be fearful listening to the sound of Jesus' heart, who was dying, and cry. *Sun Myung Moon 1/26/1958*

Jesus could not speak all that he wanted. However, he did not live only for his own purpose. While he was doing various difficult things, such as the work of a carpenter for thirty-odd years, he silently traveled the course of sacrifice for the sake of the will. From the moment he began the three-year course of his public life until the moment he died on the cross at Golgotha, there was no moment when Jesus lived for his own sake. He did not forget, even for a moment, that he had the historical mission to introduce the situation and heart of God to the earth. Jesus wanted to unveil this heart to the people of that time...

Not only that, Jesus understood that for four thousand years, countless spirits in the spirit world had been moaning and waiting for the appearance of the Messiah who could liberate them. He also knew that he was the only one who could fulfill their wishes. Furthermore, when Jesus looked at the humanity of that time, living in the hell-like earthly world, the many lives who were imprisoned and struggling fiercely inside the iron chambers of death, impatiently awaiting their liberation from the miserable environment, his heart burned in an indescribable way. We must understand that the Jesus whom we now believe in shed tears for the sake of all people of the earth and the spirits who are moaning inside the hell of the spirit world. He shed tears while fathoming the historical situation and heart of God. *Sun Myung Moon 3/23/1958*

God finally found and lifted Jesus, the one person who could fathom His situation and share His heart. However, it was not to end there. It was God's ardent desire that He could make His situation and heart known to humanity through Jesus. *Sun Myung Moon 3/23/1958*

Even if you are not aware of all the minute details of the course of history, the one thing you should have is the heart of Jesus, who came restore all things of the universe. You have to have the determination to cling to the world and fight, after understanding the heart of Jesus. *Sun Myung Moon 3/23/1958*

The religion that can connect with the ultimate world of heart should be one that can teach us in detail about God's most sorrowful state. God is not just feeling happy and wonderful; on the contrary, His plight is a deeply sad one. He has been mistreated and is overflowing with bitter grief. A religion must appear that can teach these things in detail. Only then can we become God's filial children. *Sun Myung Moon 10/28/1962*

How grieved God was that His enemy deprived Him of His throne! You should know His history of sorrow at not being able to become the God of glory. Although He is the King of His nation and King of the universe, He has been mistreated as if He were dead. He was robbed of His ideal and His loving children and our world has fully become His enemy's plaything. *Sun Myung Moon 10/21/1979*

Because there has never been a unified people or sovereign nation that God could govern, He could never manifest His authority and dignity as the all-knowing and almighty God. We have to know clearly our obligation as the sons and daughters, children of filial piety, loyal patriots and upright men and women of the Unification Movement, to relieve God's distress and comfort His sorrowful heart. Jesus said, "You will know the truth and the truth will make you free!" Those who know will be liberated! I am teaching this to you clearly. *Sun Myung Moon 5/18/1972*

How many tears have you shed for God? Have you ever struggled to seek out the path upon which you would suffer God's own pain and toil on His behalf, even though your own limbs might be torn off? You have never tried. In seeking to become God's children, you have to shed tears for the purpose of the whole. When you meet Him, your tears should gush out without ceasing as you comfort Him, saying, "Father, how great was Your sorrow upon losing me, Your son, and our first ancestors! Too many times throughout history until the present day have You suffered humiliation, pain and extreme hardship from their descendants!" *Sun Myung Moon 11/18/1971*

Think about how much time I have spent in prison, more than five years in all. Think about how rain dripping from a gutter will gradually make a hole in a rock. None of you would know how bitterly I wept as I gazed upon those drops of water, thinking how much I wished that the teardrops of my love could bore a hole through the rock of anguish embedded in God's heart! Gazing upon a flowing stream I thought how wonderful it would be if this stream could be pristine water, serving God so that He could come and bathe in it! How wonderful it would be if I could be a child who could prepare such a home or resting place for God! Unless you experience that deep world of heart, you have nothing to do with God. *Sun Myung Moon 1/1/1989*

Because none of you knows the reality of the spirit world, all of you get tired even though you offer jungsung[26] along the course of faith. However, all of you must know that the center of the spirit world is God and that God is our Father. More than anyone else, our Father stands in the closest and most unbreakable and fateful relationship with us. If I tell you what the desire of the Father is, it is the liberation of your family, and yet, not just your family alone. The issue of liberating the family of the whole of mankind is what is clogging Father's mind, even at this very moment. I can say that it is like a wall, or even like a wound that gives Father acute pain because he is unable to circulate freely (like blood through the body). *Sun Myung Moon 1/5/1999*

We have to understand how close Father's heart is to God. Then by coming close to Father we can come close to God. *Sun Myung Moon 5/24/2003*

CHAPTER 4

Christ is the hope of our soul

The road to Emmaus

Now behold, two of them were traveling that same day to a village called Emmaus, which was seven miles from Jerusalem. And they talked together of all these things which had happened. So it was, while they conversed and reasoned, that Jesus himself drew near and went with them. But their eyes were restrained, so that they did not know him.

And he said to them, "What kind of conversation is this that you have with one another as you walk and are sad?"

Then the one whose name was Cleopas answered and said to him, "Are you the only stranger in Jerusalem, and have you not known the things which happened there in these days?"

And he said to them, "What things?"

So they said to him, "The things concerning Jesus of Nazareth, who was a prophet mighty in deed and word before God and all the people, and how the chief priests and our rulers delivered him to be condemned to death, and crucified him. But we were hoping that it was he who was going to redeem Israel. Indeed, besides all this, today is the third day since these things happened. Yes, and certain women of our company, who arrived at the tomb early, astonished us. When they did not find his body, they came saying that they had also seen a vision of angels who said he was alive. And certain of those who were with us went to the tomb and found it just as the women had said; but him they did not see."

Then he said to them, "O foolish ones, and slow of heart to believe in all that the prophets have spoken! Ought not the Christ to have suffered these things and to enter into his glory?" And beginning at Moses and all the Prophets, he expounded to them in all the Scriptures the things concerning himself.

Then they drew near to the village where they were going, and he indicated that he would have gone farther. But they constrained him, saying, "Abide with us, for it is toward evening, and the day is far spent." And he went in to stay with them.

Now it came to pass, as he sat at the table with them, that he took bread, blessed and broke it, and gave it to them. Then their eyes were opened and they knew him; and he vanished from their sight.

And they said to one another, "Did not our heart burn within us while he talked with us on the road, and while he opened the Scriptures to us?" *Luke 24:13-32*

One daughter's testimony

Amanda was struggling in her marriage; constant fighting with her husband over matters large and small was taking its toll. She felt completely alone even as she was tending to their three small children. Angry and resentful, she felt estranged from God, Jesus, and True Father. She was having give and take with dark thoughts, and sometimes felt closer to Satan than to God.

Then one night she had a vivid dream; she was standing, but her spirit was broken and defeated. Eyes cast down, enveloped in despondency, she looked up to see the devil standing a stone's throw away from her. A smiling, malevolent presence, he calmly gestured, beckoning her towards him. As she began walking, True Father suddenly appeared in front of her, blocking her path to Satan. Brilliant, white light emanated from his spirit body; she was overwhelmed by the powerful waves of love rolling towards her. Speaking in a strong, confident voice, Father said "Leave her alone, devil! She is my daughter, not yours. She belongs to me! Be gone!" The devil abruptly disappeared, and Amanda was left standing next to Father, secure and enveloped in golden waves of love.

When Amanda awoke, she felt a deep sense of peace. Father had rescued her from the arms of Satan! A deep warmth tingled through her entire body as she realized that she unequivocally belonged to her beloved True Father. Her marriage was not instantly healed, but by knowing she was loved unconditionally by the King of Kings, she could find new hope to love and respect the man given to her by God. *Anonymous*

Commentary

The two men travelling to Emmaus were sorely dejected by the news that their Redeemer had been crucified. It had been three days since his death, and his body had mysteriously disappeared from the tomb. But then, unexpectedly, Jesus appeared and began walking alongside them. He lovingly chastised the two travelers for their faithless attitude. As he traveled, talked, and broke bread with them, they were transformed. His presence filled their hearts with hope that changed their lives forever. When Jesus later vanished before their eyes, they were left in a different state than before their time with the resurrected Savior.

Having a genuine encounter with Jesus radically renews us. His presence brings us fresh optimism as we experience the living waters of his love and truth. In the story of Amanda, we witness how a woman is liberated from despair by the saving love of Christ. When she thought her soul was lost, Father appeared, claiming her as his precious daughter.

By reciprocating Christ's love for us, we gain the power to return to God. Reverend Moon explained how loving Jesus can free us from Satan:

The reason Jesus said, "You must love me more than anyone else," is not because he wanted to receive love for himself. If human beings believed in those words and loved Jesus, he could grasp them with a force stronger than the force that is holding them in the realm of Satan and elevate them to the position where they could give and receive the original love with God. For this purpose, he said, "Love me more than anyone else." These words are revolutionary words of prophecy.[27]

Christ is the one ready to comfort us in our suffering; he embraces us in our loneliness. His love assures us that we will be wholly healed. When Jesus suffered the cross, when Father endured the seven deaths and resurrections,[28] they were taking the punishment that should have been ours. They were saying to all of us, "God loves you unconditionally and so do I. I am offering myself in your place." Christ cherishes us in a way that is beyond our comprehension. We begin to perceive the depth of God's love when we contemplate his son's sacrifice. Although we are totally undeserving, Christ freely offers us the grace and forgiveness that only he has the ability to bestow.

When we open our hearts to receive his love and mercy, our hearts become infused with gratitude and hope for the future. We may not know all the whys of our existence, but we can remain optimistic because God promised us He would never leave or forsake us. He is the same yesterday, today, and tomorrow. God is the rock you can stand on without doubt or fear.

Christ encourages us to maintain our vision and aspirations regardless of the circumstances. He tells us to discipline ourselves and aspire for something that does not yet exist. He quietly requests that we place our trust in him. When we pray for our loved ones in troubled times, God asks us for an even greater belief in His mercy and goodness.

Sustaining hope is often not easy; it requires patience and perseverance. But by placing our faith in God, we find the strength to press on through trials by fixing our thoughts on what Christ has promised us in the gospel.

Billy Graham explained that Jesus' resurrection "points us beyond the tragedy of the Cross to the hope of the empty tomb. It tells us that there is hope for eternal life, for Christ has conquered death. It also tells us that God has triumphed over evil and death and hell. This is our hope and it can be your hope as well."[29]

Reverend Moon could give us hope in the seven deaths and resurrections he endured during his lifetime. Perhaps the worst of these experiences was the two years and eight months he spent in the Hungnam concentration camp. Arrested in 1948, he was given a hasty trial and received a five-year sentence for preaching the gospel in newly-communist North Korea. He recalled the events ensuing his conviction:

I was led away from the court back to jail after receiving my sentence, I shook my handcuffs in front of the members of my congregation, and they made a clear and resonating sound. I still cannot forget how I waved goodbye to them with those handcuffs loudly clanking together. In that moment, it was as if a historic movie were being created for future generations. That moment would become an explosive foundation for countless young people in future generations to pledge their determination. Singing songs of hope for tomorrow is more powerful than singing of the sadness of today. The heart can always be bigger if it is filled with hope for tomorrow, rather than bitterness over the injustices of today. It didn't matter how evil the enemy was that placed handcuffs on my wrists that day.[30]

Whether enduring the cross at Golgotha or the prison in Hungnam, Christ was unwavering in his love for God and humankind. His complete trust in God, his total selflessness defies our worldly perspective and we are left in humble awe. What wondrous love is this?

We are drawn to Christ like a child to their parent. The Messiah's irrepressible hope sustains us in the most difficult of times, and seeks to lift us up into the waiting arms of God. Shall we let him?

Scripture

For there is hope for a tree,
If it is cut down, that it will sprout again,
And that its tender shoots will not cease.
Though its root may grow old in the earth,
And its stump may die in the ground,
  Yet at the scent of water it will bud
And bring forth branches like a plant. *Job 14:7-9*

But the eyes of the Lord are on those who fear Him,
on those whose hope is in His steadfast love,
that He may deliver them from death,
and keep them alive in famine.
We wait in hope for the Lord; He is our help and shield.
In Him our hearts rejoice, for we trust in His holy name.
May Your steadfast love be with us, Lord,
even as we put our hope in You. *Psalm 33:18-22*

Why are you cast down, O my soul, and why are you in turmoil within me? Hope in God; for I shall again praise Him, my salvation and my God. *Psalm 43:5*

You are my hiding place and my shield; I hope in Your word. *Psalm 119:115*

Hope deferred makes the heart sick, but a desire fulfilled is a tree of life. *Proverbs 13:12*

But those who wait on the Lord
Shall renew their strength;
They shall mount up with wings like eagles,
They shall run and not be weary,
They shall walk and not faint. *Isaiah 40:31*

Fear not, for I am with you; be not dismayed, for I am Your God; I will strengthen you, I will help you, I will uphold you with My righteous right hand. *Isaiah 41:10*

"For I know the thoughts that I think toward you," says the Lord, "thoughts of peace and not of evil, to give you a future and a hope. Then you will call upon Me and go and pray to Me, and I will listen to you. And you will seek Me and find Me, when you search for Me with all your heart." *Jeremiah 29:11-13*

Through the Lord's mercies we are not consumed,
Because His compassions fail not.
They are new every morning;
Great is Your faithfulness.
"The Lord is my portion," says my soul,
"Therefore I hope in Him!" *Lamentations 3:22-24*

Rejoice in hope, be patient in tribulation, be constant in prayer. *Romans 12:12*

May the God of hope fill you with all joy and peace as you trust in Him, so that you may overflow with hope by the power of the Holy Spirit. *Romans 15:13*

So we do not lose heart. Though our outer self is wasting away, our inner self is being renewed day by day. For this light momentary affliction is preparing for us an eternal weight of glory beyond all comparison, as we look not to the things that are seen but to the things that are unseen. For the things that are seen are transient, but the things that are unseen are eternal. *2 Corinthians 4:16-18*

Now faith is the assurance of things hoped for, the conviction of things not seen. *Hebrews 11:1*

But since we belong to the day, let us be sober, having put on the breastplate of faith and love, and for a helmet the hope of salvation. *1 Thessalonians 5:8*

Blessed be the God and Father of our Lord Jesus Christ! According to his great mercy, he has caused us to be born again to a living hope through the resurrection of Jesus Christ from the dead, to an inheritance that is imperishable, undefiled, and unfading, kept in heaven for you, who by God's power are being guarded through faith for a salvation ready to be revealed in the last time. In this you rejoice, though now for a little while, if necessary, you have been grieved by various trials, so that the tested genuineness of your faith—more precious than gold that perishes though it is tested by fire—may be found to result in praise and glory and honor at the revelation of Jesus Christ. *1 Peter 1:3-6*

God works through the person who lives for the future, studies for the future, fights for the future, hopes for the future, and goes forward to make a new future. *Sun Myung Moon 6/19/1973*

The highest hope of a human being is to reconnect with God. *Sun Myung Moon 7/29/1973*

Because God continues to have eternal hope, today we too continue to cherish an eternal hope. *Sun Myung Moon 6/6/1956*

A person entertains all kinds of hope in his life. However, in the end he runs into death. He passes away having left behind all the hopes he had fostered. Although he wandered through life seeking new hope, wishing to live today and tomorrow, when he runs into death he goes the last path in despair. Self-centered people may seem to have hope, but they lack the hope that can carry them over the hill of death. As they approach the time of their death, they lose all hope and just fade away. Shall we die in this manner? Or shall we find the one hope by which we can go beyond death, scoffing at death and even delighting in it? This is the most crucial question for human beings living on earth today. Heaven has made limitless efforts to equip earthly people with a hope that transcends death, in order that they might live with their eyes fixed on the eternal world. Therefore, people who lead a religious life should not live embracing earthly hopes, but should live entertaining the hope of transcending death. They should dream of a world where hope springs eternal. *Sun Myung Moon 3/22/1959*

May we go forth with a bold and vibrant attitude as God's hopeful sons and daughters, going towards the nation of peace, the peace of the Kingdom of Heaven. *Sun Myung Moon 8/16/1970*

Ask the rising sun what it hopes to see here on earth. It will reply that it wants to see a man and woman who are absolutely perfected in love, and that's why it has been shining for thousands of years. If you have a way to ask the birds who are whistling in the morning, they will say they want to see the day when the kingship of God's love is established here on earth. All things of creation are un-corrupted, so they will have the correct answer if you ask them. *Sun Myung Moon 4/1/1979*

We must help God to be a God of hope so that He will not see only despair and pain here on earth. In the shortest time the world shall come under the kingship of God, and when God has real hope of that He will truly be joyful. Just think, you are sons and daughters of God; He is our living God and Father. He has been brokenhearted for 6,000 years, without even one good day or hopeful spring. Don't you want to be the son of filial piety who can welcome that Father to the cosmic spring? If you have a longing to live for that goal it is a great blessing for you and the greatest success of your life. Nothing else in your life could be more extraordinary or precious than to find this truth and the place to practice it. *Sun Myung Moon 4/1/1979*

Although I am not handsome, I have an unchanging hope, and that is to pursue God's will. *Sun Myung Moon 5/8/1983*

While enduring suffering and hardship, we keep a hopeful spirit. We get down on our knees and pray, "O God, please let our hope be realized." We inherited this spirit from our forebears, and we will pass it down to our descendants. We are not like ordinary people, who when facing the same circumstances, would easily blame God saying, "If God exists, why does He let His people suffer?" *Sun Myung Moon 9/1/1987*

"Blessing of Glory"[31]

Now the light of glory arises, like the sun that shines on high;
Now awaken into freedom, O revive, you spirits, O revive!
Wake the mountains and the valleys;
bring alive the springs of the earth.
Light the world forever with the light of your rebirth.
Light the world forever with the light of your rebirth.

We are called to bring back the glory to the life of God above;
Now the Lord in His greatness fills the universe with tender love,
Ever seeking souls awakened, ever calling them to be free.
How shall I attend Him who is calling to me?
How shall I attend Him who is calling to me?

From the dark of death I awaken and rejoice to live in grace;
When the one who came to save me holds me tenderly in
His embrace,
I rejoice to feel the comfort of the love He has for me.
What a blessing of glory to rejoice eternally!
What a blessing of glory to rejoice eternally!

Now He lifts me up to embrace me in the blessing that is mine;
What a blessing to receive Him in a love so tender and divine;
How can I return the blessing though in all my life I will try,
I can never stop feeling how unworthy am I.
I can never stop feeling how unworthy am I!

CHAPTER 5

Christ endured unspeakable suffering with an unchanging heart

Jesus gave his life for our sins

Now as they led him away, they laid hold of a certain man, Simon a Cyrenian, who was coming from the country, and on him they laid the cross that he might bear it after Jesus.

And a great multitude of the people followed him, and women who also mourned and lamented him. But Jesus, turning to them, said, "Daughters of Jerusalem, do not weep for me, but weep for yourselves and for your children. For indeed the days are coming in which they will say, 'Blessed are the barren, wombs that never bore, and breasts which never nursed!' Then they will begin to say to the mountains, 'Fall on us!' and to the hills, 'Cover us! For if they do these things in the green wood, what will be done in the dry?' "

There were also two others, criminals, led with him to be put to death. And when they had come to the place called Calvary, there they crucified him, and the criminals, one on the right hand and the other on the left. Then Jesus said, "Father, forgive them, for they do not know what they do."

And they divided his garments and cast lots. And the people stood looking on. But even the rulers with them sneered, saying, "He saved others; let him save himself if he is the Christ, the chosen of God."

The soldiers also mocked him, coming and offering him sour wine, and saying, "If you are the King of the Jews, save yourself."

And an inscription also was written over him in letters of Greek, Latin, and Hebrew: THIS IS THE KING OF THE JEWS.

Then one of the criminals who were hanged blasphemed him, saying, "If you are the Christ, save yourself and us."

But the other, answering, rebuked him, saying, "Do you not even fear God, seeing you are under the same condemnation? And we indeed justly, for we receive the due reward of our deeds; but this man has done nothing wrong." Then he said to Jesus, "Lord, remember me when you come into your kingdom."

And Jesus said to him, "Assuredly, I say to you, today you will be with me in Paradise."

Now it was about the sixth hour, and there was darkness over all the earth until the ninth hour. Then the sun was darkened, and the veil of the temple was torn in two. And when Jesus had cried out with a loud voice, He said, "Father, into your hands I commit my spirit." Having said this, he breathed his last.

So when the centurion saw what had happened, he glorified God, saying, "Certainly this was a righteous man!" And the whole crowd who came together to that sight, seeing what had been done, beat their breasts and returned. But all his acquaintances, and the women who followed him from Galilee, stood at a distance, watching these things. *Luke 23:26-49*

So that we could stand righteous

One day I had a vision, and Father's face was shining like ten thousand suns. This vision was so brilliant, I could not approach it, so to speak. At the same time, I saw Father's body in hell, in prison. I could see that his spirit was in hell. His body was in prison; his spirit was in hell. In hell, there were demons ripping souls apart. And Father was shouting at demons, "Take my body instead, let my children go!" Then the demons would cast down the flesh that they were eating and devouring, and grab Father and split him apart. When I saw this vision I really had a spiritual breakthrough. I realized that Father went through the imprisonments, the six life and death tortures and tribulations--I realized that he willingly went the way of being tortured for me--instead of some kind of detached suffering. It was suffering for the sake of my own salvation, my family's salvation, so that we could stand righteous before God. Because of that indemnity that Father had to pay, I was inspired to call it the seven deaths and resurrections. A Father's love is a love that will not only lay their life down for their friends, but lay their life down again and again and again and again and again and again and again for their children.[32]

Reverend Hyung Jin Sean Moon, Second King of Cheon Il Guk

Commentary

The consonance of heart between Jesus and True Father is evident in their mutual willingness to endure unbearable hardship with an unchanging, unstoppable love for God and humankind.

True Father shared that when Jesus was being nailed to the cross, he held no grudge against his betrayers. Rather, with a desperate heart, he lowered his head toward Heaven and felt deeply apologetic.[33]

How can we understand such a heart? From a humanistic perspective, Jesus' attitude makes no sense. For what should he feel sorry? Jesus had devoted his entire life to loving and teaching the people of Israel. Virtually every moment of his life was spent serving God and humankind. He fully realized his position as Savior and did his utmost to deliver God's children trapped in sin. His reward was to be crucified by the very people he sought to deliver. As he hung on that wooden stake, soldiers were gambling for his clothes. The crowd which had gathered, yelled, "If you are the king of the Jews, save yourself!" The criminal hanging beside him echoed their hateful taunts, challenging Jesus to free himself if he really was the Messiah.

Looking down from the cross at the scene before him, the Savior's heart must have been deeply grieved. But even in his agony, Jesus' concern was for those he had come to save. True Father elucidated:

Jesus knew God as his father, but what kind of father did he know Him to be? When Jesus wore the crown of thorns, he felt that God was wearing a crown of thorns that was a thousand times more painful than his. When he was being nailed to the cross, he realized that God was experiencing his pain thousands of times over. Even when the spear pierced his side, he accepted it as if it were deserved since he knew that Heavenly Father had continued to struggle for His children in spite of pain much greater than his. That is why he could not hold a grudge and sorrow in his heart. He was determined not to leave a grudge and sorrow in his heart in front of humanity in spite of his pain. Although he was in a position to hold unimaginable rage and vengeance toward his enemy, he could not do so when thinking about what Heavenly Father had endured. Jesus had to overcome his own sorrow because he had come to save sorrowful humanity. He had to overcome his own pain and death because he had come to resolve the pain and death of mankind. Because he was like this, Jesus was the Savior. Because mankind had already lost its life, he had to be in a position never to condemn God even if he lost his life or had to give up all desires. We should realize that Jesus was able to become the savior of life who had taken on God's heart because he accepted this.[34]

It was because of Jesus' relationship with God that he did not hold on to resentment. To be God's son and possess His blood lineage meant that Jesus felt and experienced everything God felt and experienced. Jesus thought that since he belonged to God and God belonged to him, his sorrow was the Father's sorrow. He felt a oneness of heart with God, who had suffered more than himself. Jesus already knew how much pain God was enduring to see His beloved Son nailed to a cross. He also felt pity for the people who ridiculed and mocked him, knowing what a miserable future awaited them as a result of murdering the Son of God.

In his lifetime, Reverend Moon was imprisoned six times in South Korea, North Korea, and the United States. At eighty-eight years of age, he also endured a helicopter crash, miraculously escaping death.

Just as Jesus was sent to the chosen people of Israel, Reverend Moon was sent to the chosen people of the Second Israel, i.e. Christianity. And just as Jewish leaders were rebellious towards Christ at his First Advent, so too were Christian leaders resistant to receiving him as the Lord at his Second Coming.

Spreading the gospel in North Korea during the mid-1940s was bearing great fruit for Reverend Moon. Membership was growing rapidly in the country where Christianity was becoming increasingly popular. Ministers of established churches, however, felt threatened by the fact that many of their parishoners were beginning to attend Reverend Moon's church. Due to their jealousy, the local clergy reported him to the communist authorities. In 1946 he was arrested and accused of being a spy for the American government in South Korea. Although Reverend Moon denied their claim by explaining that he had come to North Korea to preach the word of God, he was held and tortured for four months.[35]

Finally, after one particularly brutal beating, he was thrown outside onto the prison grounds. When his followers came to visit, they were shocked to discover him nearly unconscious, half dead from the torture, his clothes stuck to his body by clotted blood. As they took him home, he was vomiting so much blood they thought he would die. His disciples carefully administered Chinese medicine to his weak, wounded body. Gradually, he began to heal. Soon after his recovery, he continued his ministry in North Korea by praying, studying the Bible, and investing completely in his followers.[36]

Due to continuing protests from Christian leaders, however, Reverend Moon was again arrested by Communist authorities less than two years later. As mentioned in the previous chapter, he was sentenced to five years of hard labor in a gulag-style labor camp in Hungnam. Hungnam was an extermination camp where prisoners were deliberately worked to death. Few lasted more than six months. Yet in that horrific environment, Reverend Moon survived for nearly three years. He recollected:

> Even when I was tortured so harshly that I threw up blood, repeatedly collapsed on the floor and finally lost consciousness, I never asked God to help me. Instead, I always prayed, "Father, don't worry. I'm not dead yet. I'm not going to die yet. I am still faithful to you. I still have a mission that I need to accomplish."[37]

In 2009, the Second King experienced firsthand the heart of Christ, after finishing a twenty-one thousand bowing condition of heart and devotion. Hyung Jin Moon had a vision of seeing True Father in hell, offering his body to the demons so that his children might be saved. It was at that moment that he realized his physical father was also his Lord and Savior. Like Jesus, True Father went to the bottom of hell for his sake. He understood that Father voluntarily withstood the torture that should have been Hyung Jin's to endure. And not just one time, but over and over again, seven times in all, for his personal salvation.

Scripture

I am poured out like water,
and all my bones are out of joint;
my heart is like wax;
it has melted within me.
My strength is dried up like a potsherd,
and my tongue clings to my jaws;
you have brought me to the dust of death.
For dogs have surrounded me;
the congregation of the wicked has enclosed me.
They pierced my hands and my feet;
I can count all my bones.
They look and stare at me.
They divide my garments among them,
and for my clothing they cast lots. *Psalm 22:14-18*

He is despised and rejected by men,
A man of sorrows and acquainted with grief.
And we hid, as it were, our faces from him;
He was despised, and we did not esteem him.
Surely he has borne our griefs
And carried our sorrows;
Yet we esteemed him stricken,
Smitten by God, and afflicted.
But he was wounded for our transgressions,
He was bruised for our iniquities;

The chastisement for our peace was upon him,
And by his stripes we are healed. *Isaiah 53:3-5*

"He committed no sin, and no deceit was found in his mouth." When they hurled their insults at him, he did not retaliate; when he suffered, he made no threats. Instead, he entrusted himself to him who judges justly. "He himself bore our sins" in his body on the cross, so that we might die to sins and live for righteousness; "by his wounds you have been healed." For "you were like sheep going astray," but now you have returned to the Shepherd and Overseer of your souls. *1 Peter 2:22-25*

For you know the grace of our Lord Jesus Christ, that though he was rich, yet for your sake he became poor, so that you through his poverty might become rich. *2 Corinthians 8:9*

And walk in love, as Christ loved us and gave himself up for us, a fragrant offering and sacrifice to God. *Ephesians 5:2*

Do everything without grumbling or arguing, so that you may become blameless and pure children of God without fault in a warped and crooked generation. Then you will shine among them like stars in the sky as you hold firmly to the word of life. And then I will be able to boast on the day of Christ that I did not run or labor in vain. *Philippians 2:14-16*

Not that I speak from want, for I have learned to be content in whatever circumstances I am. *Philippians 4:11*

And whenever you stand praying, forgive, if you have anything against anyone, so that your Father also who is in heaven may forgive you your trespasses. *Mark 11:25*

And after you have suffered a little while, the God of all grace, who has called you to His eternal glory in Christ, will himself restore, confirm, strengthen, and establish you. *1 Peter 5:10*

Let all bitterness and wrath and anger and clamor and slander be put away from you, along with all malice. *Ephesians 4:31*

Let this mind be in you which was also in Christ Jesus, who, being in the form of God, did not consider it robbery to be equal with God, but made himself of no reputation, taking the form of a bondservant, and coming in the likeness of men. And being found in appearance as a man, he humbled himself and became obedient to the point of death, even the death of the cross. Therefore God also has highly exalted him and given him the name which is above every name, that at the name of Jesus every knee should bow, of those in heaven, and of those on earth, and of those under the earth, and that every tongue should confess that Jesus Christ is Lord, to the glory of God the Father. *Philippians 2:5-11*

See to it that no one fails to obtain the grace of God; that no "root of bitterness" springs up and causes trouble, and by it many become defiled... *Hebrews 12:15*

Even as we endure and bear up under difficulty, we should be thankful and sing hymns. God may be on His way to visit us, but if He sees that we are enduring not thankfully but with bitterness, He will turn back. With what do we need to endure? A thankful spirit! Without a thankful spirit, we cannot endure. And even if we do endure, if we do not have a thankful heart, God cannot be with us. *Sun Myung Moon 5/4/1971*

What was the Fall? [The archangel] compared himself to everyone from a self-centered viewpoint; this led to complaint. Complaint led to rebellion. Therefore, complaint is not permissible for believers. To complain is essentially to attack God. But as we human beings have to repay God, complaining to God is absolutely unacceptable. My life up until now has been like that. I could never be a complainer, even though I was put in prison and tortured to the point of vomiting blood. Even though the entire world opposes me, I am grateful, knowing that it is severing my relationship with Satan's realm. It is natural that we receive opposition as long as the enemy's realm exists. There-fore, let us not complain. Let us be grateful for everything and every circumstance, and let us go our way in silence. *Sun Myung Moon 9/11/1972*

Today God is examining us, looking at whether our hearts are truly thankful. It is like in a court-room: when a crim-inal is being sentenced, if he or she accepts the sentence with gratitude, the judge and even the prosecutor will want to show mercy and reduce the penalty. *Sun Myung Moon 2/1/2007*

To live with gratitude — there is nothing else. If some of us were given wives who are inadequate, still we can be grateful that Thou has given us such wives, for we can serve them throughout our life. If our children be-come the cross of our life, still we can be grateful that through them Thou provideth us a way to bear a cross. Though circumstances drive us to the pits of despair in situations we cannot control, though we may col-lapse, let it be reckoned as an opportunity to reaf-firm our gratitude to Thee as Thy sons and daughters. *Sun Myung Moon 3/14/1970*

Father! Please enable me to feel grateful for all the grace Thou hast given, that a day could come when I could meet Thee—a day like today. *Sun Myung Moon 1/9/1971*

What is the essence of a life of faith? It is a heart of gratitude to God. That heart is the basis by which we can transcend the relationship ordinary fallen people have with God and enter a higher relationship with God—that of oneness. Should we thank God only when we are prospering? No. Did God care for us only when things were going well for Him? No. The more difficult the situation, the more firm was God's determination, regardless of the suffering, to labor and struggle on our behalf. Therefore, today, to properly serve God as our Father, we should demonstrate our gratitude to Him when we are going through difficult situations rather than easy ones. When you understand this principle, you will be able to give gratitude to God even when your path requires you to bear a very heavy cross. *Sun Myung Moon 2/16/1970*

Father, may we be Thy children who ask ourselves
whether we start the day as Thine,
and having arrived at this moment, are Thine.
Yet have we spent this day with worldly minds?
When we remember Thy concern for us,
we know we must spend this day valuably.
When we lay down in bed, exhausted,
do we have any regrets of things left undone?
May we not go to bed until we have repented with tears...
Though my body is exhausted,
at the point when I can hold on no more,

I must think that in Thy longing for me:
Thou hast overcome suffering harsher than mine.
I recognize that only by overcoming this suffering
can I become a son or daughter who can comfort Thy
sorrowful past;
therefore I shall purify myself on the path to becoming
Thy child,
and offer myself completely as a sacrifice before Thee.

Sun Myung Moon 3/14/1970

CHAPTER 6

Christ taught us to love because God is love

No condemnation in love

The teachers of the law and the Pharisees brought in a woman caught in adultery. They made her stand before the group and said to Jesus, "Teacher, this woman was caught in the act of adultery. In the Law Moses commanded us to stone such women. Now what do you say?" They were using this question as a trap, in order to have a basis for accusing him.

But Jesus bent down and started to write on the ground with his finger. When they kept on questioning him, he straightened up and said to them, "Let any one of you who is without sin be the first to throw a stone at her." Again he stooped down and wrote on the ground.

At this, those who heard began to go away one at a time, the older ones first, until only Jesus was left, with the woman still standing there. Jesus straightened up and asked her, "Woman, where are they? Has no one condemned you?"

"No one, sir," she said.

"Then neither do I condemn you," Jesus declared. "Go now and leave your life of sin." *John 8:3-11*

Loving your enemy

"Abba, when you were in prison, what did you talk to the guards about?"

"What do you mean?"

"When they tortured you, was there anything you said to them?"

"I told them that they needed to know Hananim."[38]

Upon hearing his response, I viscerally saw an image of a man swinging a bloodied baton, as if I was watching a movie. The camera caught this man's wicked grin, as if he was saying, "Yeah, I want you dead!" I could hardly see his hand as it flashed towards the camera, once, twice, three times. I closed my eyes. All I heard was profanities and thuds, like meat being beaten, and flattened. I winced at the imagined pain, and as I opened my eyes, I could even see dark ruddy droplets floating through the air--they fell with the inevitability of silenced horror, creating splatter art as they dissolved onto the wretched floor.

When I reflect on what Abonim had to endure, I am overwhelmed by the humbling feeling that any of my difficulties or hindrances are quite paltry, at best. I don't know how he did it. I can't fully grasp how he could manifest a "response" of forgiveness and compassion to those who bombarded him with malice, literally beating him to a pulp, tossing him out like discarded leftovers.

It's remarkable what he has in his reservoir of life experience. I do sometimes, get a glimpse of his scarred body when he receives acupressure, or electro-stem. He doesn't like to get pity over them you know. The shiny, repaired gashes and cuts glisten under the lights, as he walks from the den to his room.

At moments like that I almost find myself asking, "What histories are behind those scars?" Each of them have their unique story of horror; each of them, a little novelette of torn flesh, but impenetrable will. You know, I sometimes find myself saying, "Abba is amazing." When I see those scars, they, in some strange way, remind me of this sentiment.

I cannot know what psychological processes Abba experienced. I cannot know the sheer emotion that accompanied each of the torture sessions. I cannot know what Abba was thinking or what words he repeated in his mind, but in some way I got a clear glimpse into his soul. I saw his authenticity.

I saw his genuine laugh and his baby-like eyes smiling. I saw his tenderness as he held my son in his arms, gently rocking him back and forth. I saw an effulgence of radiance in the way he extended his scarred hand with loving compassion towards the man who ordered his death--embracing him as a brother.

This is an incredible message of forgiveness and almost literally divine compassion. To forgive and even love the man who wants to murder you is undoubtedly one of the most difficult religious and spiritual developments and growths to actualize. To ask for no explanation or apology, but to simply and deeply love was what Abonim practiced.[39]

Reverend Hyung Jin Sean Moon, Second King of Cheon Il Guk

Commentary

Love is the highest desire of humankind because it is the highest desire of God. God has no need for power, wealth, or knowledge, because He is the origin and true owner of those things. What God is unable to possess on His own, however, is love. For love to exist, there must be free exchange between subject and object. When God made Adam and Eve, it was because He wanted children who would freely choose to love Him.

Centering on Adam, God desired to experience the many facets of love existent within the family. Reverend Moon taught that God wanted to even perfect His own heart through loving Adam, Eve, and their children. Although the Fall prevented this from happening, God's desire has never changed.

As we examine the words and actions of Jesus, we find a window into the fatherly, forgiving heart of God. Jesus demonstrated great compassion in his skillful handling of the adulterous woman and the Pharisees. He put love into action by directing the Jewish teachers to stop condemning others and instead change their own self-righteous attitudes. After rescuing the woman from physical death, Jesus then gave her the words she needed to save her spiritual life.

Christ accepts us as we are, but he loves us too much to leave us alone. He guides us to shift our focus from criticizing others to rooting out the sin and selfishness in our own hearts. In that way, our spiritual arteries and veins become clearer, and God's love can more freely flow within us.

Just as Jesus prayed for the people who placed him on the cross, Reverend Moon told his torturers that they needed to know Hananim. Rejected by the North Korean pastors he had come to serve and teach, Reverend Moon had to pay the bitter price of their defiance by undergoing imprisonment and torture at the hands of Communist prison guards. Just like Jesus, he always lived as God's son of unwavering filial piety. Rather than focusing on his own miserable situation, the young pastor sought to comfort God's heart by showing divine benevolence towards those who were ignorant of the evilness of their deeds.

Christ teaches us to love because he has the same nature as his Father. In every moment of our lives, Christ wants to show us that there is only one God, a God of love. God's love flowing between two individuals has the power to unite them into one. Love is at the center of everything and is the most powerful force in the universe. Because Christ is fully one with the Father's heart, then he is the spiritual axis around which the universe turns. Jesus and True Father encourage us at every step, every turn, to love

God and love our neighbor. The more time we spend with Christ and his Word, the more we can have a mind through which he thinks, a voice through which he speaks, and a heart through which he loves.

Scripture

O Lord, You have searched me and known me.
You know my sitting down and my rising up;
You understand my thought afar off.
You comprehend my path and my lying down,
And are acquainted with all my ways.
For there is not a word on my tongue,
But behold, Lord, You know it altogether.
You have hedged me behind and before,
And laid Your hand upon me.
Such knowledge is too wonderful for me;
It is high, I cannot attain it.
Where can I go from Your Spirit?
Or where can I flee from Your presence?
If I ascend into heaven, You are there;
If I make my bed in hell, behold, You are there.
If I take the wings of the morning,
And dwell in the uttermost parts of the sea,
Even there Your hand shall lead me,
And Your right hand shall hold me.
If I say, "Surely the darkness shall fall on me,"

Even the night shall be light about me;
Indeed, the darkness shall not hide from You,
But the night shines as the day;
The darkness and the light are both alike to You.
For You formed my inward parts;
You covered me in my mother's womb.
I will praise You, for I am fearfully and wonderfully made;
Marvelous are Your works,
And that my soul knows very well.
My frame was not hidden from You,
When I was made in secret,
And skillfully wrought in the lowest parts of the earth.
Your eyes saw my substance, being yet unformed.
And in Your book they all were written,
The days fashioned for me,
When as yet there were none of them.
How precious also are Your thoughts to me, O God!
How great is the sum of them!
If I should count them, they would be more in number
than the sand;
When I awake, I am still with You... *Psalm 139:1-18*

But now thus says the Lord,
He who created you, O Jacob,
He who formed you, O Israel:
Fear not, for I have redeemed you;
I have called you by name, you are mine.

When you pass through the waters, I will be with you;
and through the rivers, they shall not overwhelm you;
when you walk through fire you shall not be burned,
and the flame shall not consume you.
For I am the Lord Your God,
the Holy One of Israel, Your Savior. *Isaiah 43:1-3*

For the mountains may depart and the hills be removed, but My steadfast love shall not depart from you, and My covenant of peace shall not be removed, says the Lord, who has compassion on you. *Isaiah 54:10*

"The most important one," answered Jesus, "is this, 'Hear, O Israel: The Lord our God, the Lord is one. Love the Lord your God with all your heart and with all your soul and with all your mind and with all your strength.' The second is this: 'Love your neighbor as yourself.' There is no commandment greater than these." *Mark 12:29-31*

For God so loved the world that He gave His only begotten Son, that whoever believes in Him should not perish but have everlasting life. *John 3:16*

As the Father has loved me, so have I loved you. Now remain in my love. If you keep my commands, you will remain in my love, just as I have kept my Father's commands and remain in His love. I have told you this so that my joy may be in you and that your joy may be complete. My command is this: Love each other as I have loved you. Greater love has no one than this: to lay down one's life for one's friends. You are my friends if you do what I command. I no longer call you servants, because a servant does not know his master's business. Instead, I have called you friends, for everything that I learned from my Father I have made known to you...This is my command: Love each other. *John 15:9-17*

If I speak in the tongues of men and of angels, but have not love, I am a noisy gong or a clanging cymbal. And if I have prophetic powers, and understand all mysteries and all knowledge, and if I have all faith, so as to remove mountains, but have not love, I am nothing. If I give away all I have, and if I deliver up my body to be burned, but have not love, I gain nothing. Love is patient and kind; love does not envy or boast; it is not arrogant or rude. It does not insist on its own way; it is not irritable or resentful... *1 Corinthians 13:1-13*

But I say to you, love your enemies and pray for those who persecute you, so that you may be sons of your Father who is in heaven; for He causes His sun to rise on the evil and the good, and sends rain on the righteous and the unrighteous. For if you love those who love you, what reward do you have? Do not even the tax collectors do the same? If you greet only your brothers, what more are you doing than others? Do not even the Gentiles do the same? *Matthew 5:44-47*

Love must be sincere. Hate what is evil; cling to what is good. Be devoted to one another in love. Honor one another above yourselves. *Romans 12:9-10*

Beloved, let us love one another, for love is from God, and whoever loves has been born of God and knows God. Anyone who does not love does not know God, because God is love. In this the love of God was made manifest among us, that God sent His only Son into the world, so that we might live through him. In this is love, not that we have loved God but that He loved us and sent His Son to be the propitiation for our sins. Beloved, if God so loved us, we also ought to love one another. No one has ever seen God; if we love one another, God abides in us and His love is perfected in us. By this we know that we abide in Him and He in us, because He has given us of His Spirit. And we have seen and testify that the Father has sent His Son to be the Savior of the world. Whoever confesses that Jesus is the Son of God, God abides in him, and he in God. So we have come to know and to believe the love that God has for us. God is love, and whoever abides in love abides in God, and God abides in him. By this is love perfected with us, so that we may have confidence for the day of judgment, because as He is so also are we in this world. There is no fear in love, but perfect love casts out fear. For fear has to do with punishment, and whoever fears has not been perfected in love. We love because he first loved us. If anyone says, "I love God," and hates his brother, he is a liar; for he who does not love his brother whom he has seen cannot love God whom he has not seen. And this commandment we have from him: whoever loves God must also love his brother. *1 John 4:7-21*

See what great love the Father has lavished on us, that we should be called children of God! And that is what we are! The reason the world does not know us is that it did not know him. Dear friends, now we are children of God, and what we will be has not yet been made known. But we know that when Christ appears, we shall be like him, for we shall see him as he is. *1 John 3:1-2*

Above everything, love one another earnestly, because love covers over many sins. *1 Peter 4:8*

No one has ever seen God, but if we love one another, God lives in union with us, and His love is made perfect in us. We are sure that we live in union with God and that He lives in union with us, because He has given us His Spirit. *1 John 4:12-13*

There is no fear in love. But perfect love drives out fear, because fear has to do with punishment. The one who fears is not made perfect in love. We love because he first loved us. *1 John 4:18-19*

Be always humble, gentle, and patient. Show your love by being tolerant with one another. Do your best to preserve the unity which the Spirit gives by means of the peace that binds you together. *Ephesians 4:2-3*

To conclude: you must all have the same attitude and the same feelings; love one another, and be kind and humble with one another. Do not pay back evil with evil or cursing with cursing; instead, pay back with a blessing, because a blessing is what God promised to give you when He called you. *1 Peter 3:8-9*

My little children, let us not love in word or in tongue, but in deed and in truth. And by this we know that we are of the truth, and shall assure our hearts before Him. For if our heart condemns us, God is greater than our heart, and knows all things. Beloved, if our heart does not condemn us, we have confidence toward God. And whatever we ask we receive from Him, because we keep His commandments and do those things that are pleasing in His sight. And this is His commandment: that we should believe on the name of His Son Jesus Christ and love one another, as He gave us commandment. *I John 3:18-23*

The greatest hope God cherishes for humankind is not for us to be wealthy or to become academics. As it is stated in the Bible, you should love the Lord your God with all your heart, and with all your soul and with all your strength. This is the First Commandment. The Second Commandment is to love your neighbor as yourself. These are amazing words. *Cheon Seong Gyeong, p.1545*

God is the Lord of love. He exists to spread love throughout the universe and make it eternal. *Sun Myung Moon 1/17/1999*

You may gaze adoringly at Jesus' face and even touch it. You may walk with Jesus and live with Jesus, as you think he would want you to live. But unless your heart is connected with Jesus' heart, it is of no use. You have to touch Jesus through the connection of heart, and live with Jesus through the heart. *Sun Myung Moon 10/2/1960*

God is the Womb of love. He is the Source of love's emotion, out of which emanates parental love, children's love, sibling love, love of kin and love of country. These different kinds of love are like branches and leaves growing from the main trunk. They are like waves that eventually turn into ripples. The further away from the Source, the fainter the emotion becomes. *Sun Myung Moon 11/8/1971*

How does it feel to experience the realm of God's love? It is like walking through a garden on a warm spring day. You see all different kinds of flowers and become intoxicated with all their fragrances. Lying on the grass, you feel something indescribable as you look up at the sky and see the towering cumulus clouds shaped like clumps of cotton. You feel your cells dancing, breathing. God's love is the wellspring of power and happiness for all beings; it endows each one with the energy of life. God's love is the absolute requirement for faith. It is the necessary element for joy, pleasure, peace, and everything else human life desires. Moreover, God's love is the principle of the spirit world. *Sun Myung Moon 9/14/1969*

If you desire love, the secret of gaining it is to pour out yourself, your life, your love, and your everything. This is the law of recreation—simply to win the heart of people. *Sun Myung Moon 12/9/1972*

You must clearly understand the ideal world will start from you as an individual when you are with God's love, which you can put into practice in your daily life in human relationships. Love will start from you reaching out to all things, as it originally started from God reaching out to you. *Sun Myung Moon 6/1/1973*

God is the Subject of heart. For this reason, God can feel limitless sorrow as well as limitless joy. Just because He is God doesn't mean that He possesses only joy and positive emotions. When God is sad, His heart of sorrow is deeper and wider than any person can ever comprehend. *Sun Myung Moon 2/12/1961*

God exists for love and lives for love. God does not live for Himself, but for love. Likewise, all things are born from love. Thus, in the world of love, there cannot be a concept that we should live for ourselves. *Sun Myung Moon 9/9/1999*

God knows everything. Omniscient and omnipotent, He is the Supreme King of knowledge and power. Omnipresent, He exists everywhere. What does God need? Diamonds? He can make them any time. Gold or jewels? No. What God needs is love. Dwelling all by Himself, would God say, "I have love and it's great" and laugh? No, there is something that God needs. God is a personal God; then He should have a mouth, shouldn't He? He also should have a nose, eyes, ears, hands and feet, a mind—and a heart. Surely, God must have them, because He is a personal God. *Sun Myung Moon, World Scripture II, p.43*

What is the origin of human beings? God's love. We were born for love. Love is the origin. Life is not the most precious thing. Our life derived from God's idea of love; therefore, love precedes life. Love is the root of life. We are born from love, grow up in love, and meet a partner for love—that should be our life. If God is the first generation, then human beings are the second generation. God always loves us, His sons and daughters, but do we experience God's love? Human beings need to experience that love if we are to become God's perfect partners. *Sun Myung Moon 3/21/1986*

Do you really love God? Do you want to make God your own personal God? God is not the God of Reverend Moon or some minister or church. You should feel: He is my God. I must love God more than anyone else. God has to become the God of ourselves. We have to start by making God our own God before we make Him our family, society, nation, or world God. We cannot enable Him to be a world God unless He is first a personal God. *Sun Myung Moon 1/1/1989*

The highest standard for Christianity and other religions is to love one's enemy. God also stands in this position according to the Principle. Therefore He cannot but love the devil, Satan. Even though Satan is the enemy of love, God must love this enemy more than He loved Adam and Eve before the Fall. Why? It is because when Eve returns to Him from the bosom of His enemy, bringing illegitimate sons and daughters with her, the Father must love them more than

He loves the children He gave birth to. Otherwise there is no way for Eve to return to her original position. Do you understand what this means? *Sun Myung Moon 8/29/1992*

Love is the air you breathe in the spirit world. Only by establishing the way of love can you become the substantiation of hope longed for by God throughout history and be welcomed everywhere you go in heaven. Thus your family is the training school enabling you to go to heaven. It is your training ground. *Sun Myung Moon 3/15/1986*

God is our father. Day and night He worries that His children may be harmed. He protects us lest troubles happen; and He defends us lest some opposing circumstances appear. He is that kind of parent. Going in search of the essence of such a parent is the way of goodness and the way of love. Human beings, as His children, need to receive God's perfect love. *Cheon Seong Gyeong, p. 334*

Why do people like and follow God? It is because God is one who gives and again gives everything for thousands of years and yet still feels ashamed. He says, "Now I can only give you this much, but wait a bit longer, and I will give you something that is many hundreds of times, many thousands of times better." This is because He is someone whose heart is not content with today's giving but promises to give better things in the future. *Cheon Seong Gyeong, p. 335*

Until now, God has given love to those people and even those tribes and nations that were near His side. He has blessed them by adding things again and again lest they should think of them as too small and not receive them. Even this was not enough, and He gave them the life of His beloved son. Even after giving over His only son to be killed, God again wants to give more love. This is why, on the day when this love is returned, all of heaven and earth will turn into an ideal Kingdom of Heaven. By the principle of love, the more love you receive, the more love you give in return. So when we give God a hundred units of love, God will return to us a thousand, ten thousand units of love. *Cheon Seong Gyeong, p. 334*

We must find true love. Then where can you find it? True love lasts forever, and remains unchanged, day or night. Something that exists for oneself alone cannot be true love. True love cannot belong to just one individual. True love belongs to all, and is jointly owned by the whole universe. True love connects the family, the society, the nation, the world, and the universe. *Cheon Seong Gyeong, p. 329*

CHAPTER 7

Christ taught us to persevere because God never gives up

The parable of the persistent widow

Then Jesus told his disciples a parable to show them that they should always pray and not give up. He said, "In a certain town there was a judge who neither feared God nor cared what people thought. And there was a widow in that town who kept coming to him with the plea, 'Grant me justice against my adversary.' For some time he refused. But finally he said to himself, 'Even though I don't fear God or care what people think, yet because this widow keeps bothering me, I will see that she gets justice, so that she won't eventually come and attack me!' "

And the Lord said, "Listen to what the unjust judge says. And will not God bring about justice for His chosen ones, who cry out to Him day and night? Will he keep putting them off? I tell you, He will see that they get justice, and quickly. However, when the Son of Man comes, will he find faith on the earth?" *Luke 18:1-8*

A truly great fisherman and a truly great fish

It was August 1977, the second consecutive summer I

had spent fishing for giant bluefin tuna with Father. This was Father's third year fishing out of Gloucester, Massachusetts. He had experimented and developed an efficient method, similar to the one used by Santiago in "The Old Man and the Sea." This method consisted of using a very specific combination of handlines, leaders, weights, floats and hooks, along with an equally specific system. He then trained us young members how to fish with his particular approach. In a short time, we had become some of the most successful bluefin fishermen in a town that prided itself on being the best.

Our hand lines consisted of six hundred feet of increasingly thinner lines, ending with a Japanese-made 8-0 tuna hook. The nylon ropes were loosely coiled in heavy plastic baskets set close to the gunwales and transom of the cockpit. Father liked six lines to be set out, one from either side of the boat, the other four trailing from the stern on floats. The baits were set at different depths, depending on the current and direction of the wind. The objective was to set the bait (usually whiting or mackerel) at the right depth and distance, in the line of drifting and sinking chum tossed from the stern.

Father had learned early on that skimping on chum meant catching fewer tuna. We would often go through one hundred pounds of chum in one day. Father was intensely focused on watching the bait, calculating how deep, how far out each piece should be put.

Brown as a berry and sporting a long-billed fishing cap, he would sit up on the flying bridge and give us directions on how to shift the position of each line as conditions changed. At the same time, he often would be meeting and talking with church leaders, but never lost his focus on fishing. Father's great concentration, and our unity with him, were the key ingredients to our success.

We had been fishing out in Stellwagen Bank since 4:30 that morning from the "New Hope," Father's 48 foot sport-fisherman. The weather was hot and still; we had already been on the water for nearly ten hours. Finally, around 2:00 in the afternoon, we hooked up. We began to fight the fish as the designated crewman grabbed the line as it flew out of its basket. The rest of us brought in the other lines and cleared the deck for what was to become a very long fight.

When a tuna is caught, it will ordinarily dive deep, and then start swimming in a clockwise direction. Mature tuna, however, have learned through experience that the best way to rid themselves of the hook is to run close to the surface and tangle the line in the rudders. This tuna stayed shallow as it swam around the boat, so we knew he must be a seasoned veteran. The powerful fish continued to run in circles, trying to find the sweet spot where he could cast off the hook. As he ran shallower still, the line fouled the rudders, forcing us to free the line on each pass. At first we could clear the line with the boat hook, guiding it away from the rudders, but as we brought the fish closer, he ran shallower, and his circuit around the boat became more frequent. It finally became necessary to un-tie the lighter line from the main line, pull it out from the rudders and retie. This momentarily left only a few feet of slack line for the crewman who was fighting the fish. If the fish made a strong run at this time he was gone.

After about an hour and a half of this, we brought the tuna close enough for Father to put a harpoon into him. Usually this finishes the fish, but this brute simply took off again. We now had two lines to clear from the rudders. After two circuits of this turmoil, we knew we were about to lose him. Someone shouted "Let's fight from the bow!" Unorthodox for sure, but Father immediately responded "Let's do it!"

We fought from the bow another three and a half hours; about halfway through this phase the leader on the hook line broke. This left us with just the harpoon to bring him in. Very carefully we coaxed the fish closer and closer. Fi-nally, the tuna wore out, and we moved back to the cockpit.

A couple more circuits and he was right along the port side. Father put three 12 gauge slugs into him to close the deal. With our rope now cinched around his tail we had our fish--but we also learned just how close a battle it had been. We discovered that the harpoon had come out early on, and its line had become tangled in the remainder of the leader. As we brought the fish on board, the hook fell out of its mouth.

At eight hundred eighty pounds, he had fought us for nearly six hours, and towed the New Hope five and a half miles from the fleet. This was a truly great fish and a truly great fight.[40]

Doug Williams

Commentary

Every parable of Jesus contains priceless truth for those who have the eyes to see and the ears to hear. In the story of the persistent widow, Jesus teaches us that perseverance is an invaluable quality necessary for victory. This parable demonstrates that prayer must be accompanied by tenacity and faithfulness to bear fruit.

Effective prayer is based on a sincere trust in God. We can fully count on Jesus to answer when, where, and how he chooses. God expects us to keep on asking, seeking, knocking, and praying until the answers come *(Matthew 7:7–8)*. To the degree that we cooperate with God in our lives, we are able to be remade into the likeness of Christ. Winning for God means that we allow Christ to recreate us as we fight. The important connection between perseverance and character can be seen in *Romans 5:3-4*, which says, "knowing that tribulation produces perseverance; and perseverance, character; and character, hope." This process requires pressing on through trials *(James 5:10-11)*. God knows that without difficulties, our faith would not be tested, and we would not grow. The means by which a snake sheds its skin and reveals a new layer underneath is not an easy one. But it is only when we obey God's word in our lives that our character can be transformed. James explains in *James 1:3-4*, "knowing that the testing of your faith produces patience. But let patience have its perfect work, that you may be perfect and complete, lacking nothing."

In *1 Peter 5:8*, the apostle Peter warns us, "Be alert and of sober mind. Your enemy the devil prowls around like a roaring lion looking for someone to devour." To keep our spiritual equilibrium, it is essential to put on our spiritual armor *(Ephesians 6:10-18)* and stay resolute in our determination to follow Christ. We can do all things through Christ who strengthens us *(Philippians 4:13)*, but it is we who must choose, on a daily basis, to "put on the Lord Jesus Christ" *(Romans 13:14)* and ask him to be Lord of our life.

Jesus' story of the persistent widow highlights the need to persevere beyond when it is comfortable, so that God may accomplish His Will through us. Having faith is essential, but we must act on that faith by using our heart, mind, and will to overcome obstacles. In order to capture the eight hundred eighty pound tuna, Father and his crew had to consistently push through each difficult problem that occurred while fighting the fish.

Perseverance centered on heartistic unity with Christ is what ultimately brings victory. Based on the crew's oneness with Father's leadership, they could eventually catch the tuna. When Jesus asked the question, "However, when the Son of Man comes, will he find faith on the earth?" at the end of the persistent widow parable, he was indicating that perseverance must be accompanied by faith in him in order to accomplish Heaven's will.

Scripture

Have I not commanded you? Be strong and courageous. Do not be frightened, and do not be dismayed, for the Lord your God is with you wherever you go. *Joshua 1:9*

But as for you, be strong and do not give up, for your work will be rewarded. *2 Chronicles 15:7*

Be strong and let your heart take courage, all you who wait for the Lord! *Psalm 31:24*

The Lord waits to be gracious to you; Therefore He exalts himself to show mercy to you. For the Lord is a God of justice; Blessed are those who wait for Him. *Isaiah 30:18*

And to those who have no might He increases strength.
Even the youths shall faint and be weary,
And the young men shall utterly fall,
But those who wait on the Lord
Shall renew their strength;

They shall mount up with wings like eagles,
They shall run and not be weary,
They shall walk and not faint.
Isaiah 40:29-31

Fear not, for I am with you; be not dismayed, for I am your God; I will strengthen you, I will help you, I will uphold you with My righteous right hand. *Isaiah 41:10*

Yea, I have spoken it, I will also bring it to pass; I have purposed it, I will also do it. *Isaiah 46:11*

Have I not commanded you? Be strong and courageous. Do not be frightened, and do not be dismayed, for the Lord your God is with you wherever you go. *Joshua 1:9*

And I am sure of this, that he who began a good work in you will bring it to completion at the day of Jesus Christ. *Philippians 1:6*

Jesus looked at them and said, "With man this is impossible, but with God all things are possible." *Matthew 19:26*

He who endures to the end will be saved. *Mark 13:13*

Until now you have asked nothing in my name. Ask, and you will receive, that your joy may be full. *John 16:24*

Rejoice in hope, be patient in tribulation, be constant in prayer. *Romans 12:12*

And I am sure of this, that he who began a good work in you will bring it to completion at the day of Jesus Christ. *Philippians 1:6*

I know how to be abased, and I know how to abound. Everywhere and in all things I have learned both to be full and to be hungry, both to abound and to suffer need. I can do all things through Christ who strengthens me. *Philippians 4:12-13*

Be strong and let your heart take courage, all you who wait for the Lord! *Psalm 31:24*

And let us not grow weary of doing good, for in due season we will reap, if we do not give up. *Galatians 6:9*

Whatever you do, work at it with all your heart, as working for the Lord, not for human masters, since you know that you will receive an inheritance from the Lord as a reward. It is the Lord Christ you are serving. *Colossians 3:23-24*

I have fought the good fight, I have finished the race, I have kept the faith. *2 Timothy 4:7*

No discipline seems pleasant at the time, but painful. Later on, however, it produces a harvest of righteousness and peace for those who have been trained by it. *Hebrews 12:11*

What was the secret of Jesus' victory over death? He lived for the sake of others and established a path of endurance through his own example. If in the Garden of Gethsemane he had said, "Father! Take this cup away from me! Please, I insist on it!" he would have lost everything. Yet instead he said, "Nevertheless, not my will, but Thy will be done." Because he endured and went on, he was victorious. That is his greatness. *Sun Myung Moon 3/2/1975*

The Bible records... that in the Last Days even people with faith will find it hard to survive. Therefore, you must endure and forebear until the very end if you are to overcome this age of chaos and become victors. *Sun Myung Moon 5/18/1958*

Our endurance should not end midway; it should go all the way. God has endured for six thousand years for this. Who is God? He is our Father. Because we inherited His flesh and blood and His virtues, we must be like Him. *Sun Myung Moon 5/4/1971*

You cannot complete your life of faith in one morning or one day. It is a lifelong path. In a life of faith, the main issue is to maintain your dedication with a constant mind and heart with a view towards eternity, beyond death. Your center core must be unchanging. No matter how difficult, sorrowful or painful, it can never change. To follow the path of faith you must discover this core in yourself, something you can never deny. *Sun Myung Moon 7/23/1972*

On your quest you will be hampered by innumerable foes, but you must fight them and fight them again, advance and advance again, clash and clash again. Thus supporting the altar of patience with your shoulders, feet, hands, torso and head, you must become a living offering who can climb over the hill of perseverance. *Sun Myung Moon 3/29/1959*

I don't want to have just watchers, those who wait for others to carry out the mission. You must carry out your own mission of restoring yourselves and restoring the whole world. I am a grave man, a serious man. I am still at war with Satan, every minute of my life. You must be so brave as I am and fight on with me working with you -- through you. *Sun Myung Moon 1/19/1973*

Whatever mistakes were made in dispensational history usually resulted from a lack of perseverance and deep thinking. Of all the creation, who would have tolerated the most and contemplated the most deeply? What kind of man? Would he be the one with power, or a man without power who had to suffer and endure? The weak man may be righteous but because he is in a powerless position, he follows the tradition of perseverance and contemplation. Such men know it is wise not to speak, so they endure. Why do they not act? They refrain in order to become better than whoever is in power and make sure by long tolerance that they are superior. They persevere for the future, regardless of the present. *Sun Myung Moon 8/27/1978*

A mature person makes effort to discover the sweet taste in all things bitter. That way, he knows their real taste. It is a law that things are sometimes up, sometimes down, as they go through their cycles. Likewise, sweet things leave a bitter taste, while bitter things have some sweetness in them. *Sun Myung Moon 8/1/1978*

Which is the good side? The good side waits for a long time, keeps patience for a long time and keeps hope for a long time. The evil side has no patience. If it is at a disadvantage, it will try to punch the other and jump to action at once. The good stays patient and endures even through struggle and frustration. Whatever comes, it maintains hope and does not fall into despair. A good person is patient and enduring not only for himself; he is also patient and enduring for those who are not patient. *Sun Myung Moon 5/21/1977*

If you are determined, then God will work. *Sun Myung Moon 12/27/1971*

CHAPTER 8

Christ asks his followers to have faith and be obedient to him

The faith of a Canaanite woman

Leaving that place, Jesus withdrew to the region of Tyre and Sidon. A Canaanite woman from that vicinity came to him, crying out, "Lord, Son of David, have mercy on me! My daughter is demon-possessed and suffering terribly."

Jesus did not answer a word. So his disciples came to him and urged him, "Send her away, for she keeps crying out after us."

He answered, "I was sent only to the lost sheep of Israel."

The woman came and knelt before him. "Lord, help me!" she said.

He replied, "It is not right to take the children's bread and toss it to the dogs."

"Yes it is, Lord," she said. "Even the dogs eat the crumbs that fall from their master's table."

Then Jesus said to her, "Woman, you have great faith! Your request is granted." And her daughter was healed at that moment. *Matthew 15:21-28*

A daughter, not a daughter-in-law

Hyung Jin nim and I were travelling with Father on his last world tour. It was July 2011, in Abuja, Nigeria. Father was speaking to an overflowing crowd of African members and international church missionaries who had flown in for the event. Over three thousand people were in attendance of what was to be Father's final visit to Africa. Father was pouring out his heart to the African brothers and sisters who sat before him with shining faces. He was moved by their joyful exuberance at seeing their True Parent in person. Members were eagerly drinking in every word, even though he had been speaking for hours. But we were on a tight schedule, and a Korean leader came up to the stage to tell him it was time to go. If we left after 12 noon it might be difficult to get our plane refueled in Iceland. But, as had happened many times in the past, Father ignored the request and continued speaking. Another Korean leader then came on stage, once again to tell him that they needed to leave posthaste. Father responded "No, no, no! This might be the last time they will see me!" Then Hyung Jin nim came on stage, pleading "Father, we have to go." "No, I'm not going!" was his reply. He gave Hyung Jin nim a slap on the face after he spoke, and then summoned me to the stage, calling "Yeonah! Yeonah!" I quickly came to the platform, not knowing why he was asking for me. The next thing I knew, Father slapped me as well. Although his hand did not hit my face very hard, I was in shock.

This was a very stressful time for me. Since becoming the International Church President in 2008, Hyung Jin nim had been the subject of criticism from people both inside and outside the church who did not want him to succeed. I knew they could easily use this public scolding of our couple as fuel for their negative fire. I shakily sat down on the stage as Father continued to speak. After about ten minutes he finished, and we briskly proceeded to make our way to the airport. Upon leaving, several people came up to me and asked if I was ok. I responded that I was fine, but in reality, I was angry and upset. I felt that I had been publically humiliated by Father slapping me before an audience of thousands watching his every move.

On the drive to the airport I was silent, trying to sleep without success. An African political leader was at the terminal to greet us when we arrived. He quickly began conversing with Father and Hyung Jin nim. Before long, the three of them were engaged in joyful conversation filled with laughter. This only served to increase my displeasure. Didn't my husband have any empathy for me, his suffering wife? Didn't he care about how I had been harshly treated?

As we boarded the private airplane, my only thought was to keep myself from crying. We were in close quarters, and any tearful outbursts were sure to be noticed by Father, who was sitting only a few feet away. And so I picked up my iPad, and proceeded to play video games for the next seven hours as we flew to Iceland. I rarely play computer games, but this was my only defense to keep the tears from coming. I couldn't talk to my husband; I was too angry to pray. I thought, if Father sees me crying, he might be even more displeased than when he had hit me. And so I focused on lining up fruits on the screen in front of me, and exploding them to dull my turbulent emotions. I played so long my shoulder became numb!

We refueled in Iceland, and finally landed home in Las Vegas. Father was vibrant and cheerful as we disembarked. Hyung Jin nim clasped his hand and said, "Father! I was so happy when you struck me back in Nigeria! You are still so strong! You have such energy and power!" Father was delighted by his son's sincere, heartfelt remarks. Me? I was still disgruntled and upset. How could my husband express such unconditional devotion?

As we were waiting at the baggage claim for our luggage, a staff member remarked to Father, "Abonim, even in a normal house, much less a royal family, fathers don't hit their daughters-in-law. Their daughters-in-law are not as close, and they can more easily become upset." Father's response? "I never hit my daughter-in-law. That was my daughter."

When he spoke those words, a huge dark cloud lifted from my heart. Father loved me as his flesh and blood daughter! He wanted no distance between us. I suddenly realized that he had struck me and Hyung Jin nim not for any selfish reason, but from the desire to teach us a deep lesson. We did not recognize the value of the living Christ spending time with disciples who dearly loved him, and who were probably seeing him for the last time. Father hoped we would have the faith to understand this simple, profound truth.

Two days later, as I was clearing Father's table after dinner, he said to me, "Yeonah, you cannot hold a grudge. I wanted to teach you--so don't hold a grudge, ok?" Somehow Father sensed that there was some unforgiveness in my heart. He spoke again:

"Don't hold any resentment against me, ok?"

"Yes, Father, I understand."

"I wanted to teach you. That's why I did what I did."

The next day, at Hoon Dook Hae, Father looked over at me, and repeated what he had said the day before: "You don't hold a grudge against me, Yeonah, ok?"

"Oh no, Father, don't worry. I don't hold any grudge against you."

I was wondering why Father had spoken the same words to me as the previous day. Upon reflection, I realized that he detected some resentment still buried in my heart, and he wanted no barriers between us. I was so grateful for his care and concern that my heart be freed from any lingering bitterness.

As I think back, I can see that this was a turning point in my life of faith. Father had made special effort to make sure I knew that he had acted in my best interests. He wanted me to overcome my resentment so that I could be free to love him.

Because of the incredible strength and power of our Father, we sometimes forget about the tender-hearted Christ who is also gentle and kind, and wants to have a close relationship with each one of us. I felt like one of the little sparrows that was not forgotten before God.

To love Christ means to trust in his goodness. My husband's example of joyful obedience was a beautiful example of absolute faith. We may not always understand in the moment why Christ is speaking or acting in a particular way, but we can obey with filial piety because we can have faith in Christ's heart of perfect love.[41]

Yeonah Lee Moon, Second Queen of Cheon Il Guk

Commentary

In both stories of chapter 8, Christ acts in a way most of us don't associate with the behavior of a Savior. We are more accustomed to a Messiah whose words and actions leave us with a feeling of indebtedness. But these two stories evoke the questions, "Why did Jesus compare the Canaanite woman to a dog?" and "Why would Reverend Moon strike his children?"

A closer study of the passage cited in Matthew reveals that Jesus' response was an expression of obedience to the Father, as well as a test of the Canaanite woman's faith. Jesus was keenly aware that his primary mission was to witness to the people of Israel. His duty before Heaven was to save the nation eagerly awaiting their Redeemer. God had spent four thousand years preparing the Jews so they would receive His only begotten son. It was for this reason the disciples urged their master to send the pleading woman away. She was not of the people God had personally raised up, but from a religious group which worshipped many gods and practiced temple prostitution.

Jesus was also testing this woman's faith in him. Would she endure his harsh words with an unchanging heart? Scripture has recorded that the Canaanite woman kept her position before Jesus and maintained her confidence in his goodness. She humbly received his words, and continued to petition and believe in her Lord. Because of her unwavering faith and obedience, Jesus praised her and healed her ailing daughter.

Hyung Jin and Yeonah Moon were also being tested by Christ when he slapped their faces. Hyung Jin delighted Father's heart by responding with unconditional praise for his parent. Upon reflection, Yeonah realized that Father had answered the higher calling of God by ignoring the requests to leave for the airport. The slap on the cheek was to teach her this deep heartistic reality he shared with Heavenly Father.

Father demonstrated great faith in Hyung Jin and Yeonah by giving them an easy opportunity to misjudge him. Although Yeonah initially deemed his treatment of her as unkind and hurtful, she broke through when she realized that Father was actually relating to her on a deeper level. He trusted her to understand his heart.

In *Matthew 18:3*, Jesus tells us that unless we change and become as little children, we cannot enter the Kingdom of Heaven. A child believes without complication; his inclination is to obey and follow his parents. Is this not the way Christ wants us to relate with him? Jesus is telling us that we need to have this simple attitude towards God our Father. After all, we are His children. We should be able to come to Him without any doubts that He loves and cares for us.

Many long-time members of the Unification Church remember the wrath of Reverend Moon. He could roar like a powerful lion, scolding and calling us to repentance. The author was in his presence on many such occasions. Knowing that the Second King had also been chastised by Father, I once asked him, "When Father harshly scolded you, did you ever feel like he didn't love you?" His response was to look at me with a gaze of incomprehension as if to say, "How could you even think such a thing?" He then shared that he would return to Father with greater devotion and attendance than before. Hyung Jin nim commented, "Father loved it when members responded like that."

When we are tested, we are being asked to remain faithful, to obey and praise God, regardless of the circumstance. Why? Because our Heavenly Father is always good, always loving, and always looking out for our best interests, whether or not we are deserving.

Maintaining a demeanor of grateful obedience to Christ in all situations is of course not easy, but this is exactly the point. It is our life-long training of how we can become more like him, the one who is always faithful and obedient to God.

The Messiah asks us to have a childlike faith. As we learn to let go and trust in him, he is free to recreate us to become our true selves.

Scripture

Now then, if you will indeed obey My voice and keep My covenant, then you shall be My own possession among all the peoples, for all the earth is Mine... *Exodus 19:5*

Now, Israel, what does the Lord your God require from you, but to fear the Lord your God, to walk in all His ways and love Him, and to serve the Lord your God with all your heart and with all your soul, and to keep the Lord's commandments and His statutes which I am commanding you today for your good? *Deuteronomy 10:12-13*

Now, therefore, fear the Lord and serve Him in sincerity and truth; and put away the gods which your fathers served beyond the River and in Egypt, and serve the Lord.

If it is disagreeable in your sight to serve the Lord, choose for yourselves today whom you will serve: whether the gods which your fathers served which were beyond the River, or the gods of the Amorites in whose land you are living; but as for me and my house, we will serve the Lord. *Joshua 24:14-15*

And I will betroth you to Me in faithfulness. Then you will know the Lord. *Hosea 2:20*

Know therefore that the Lord your God, He is God, the faithful God, who keeps His covenant and His loving kindness to a thousandth generation with those who love Him and keep His commandments... *Deuteronomy 7:9*

Trust in the Lord with all your heart,
And lean not on your own understanding;
In all your ways acknowledge Him,
And He shall direct your paths. *Proverbs 3:5-6*

O love the Lord, all you His godly ones! The Lord preserves the faithful and fully recompenses the proud doer. *Psalm 31:23*

Trust in the Lord forever, for in God the Lord, we have an everlasting Rock. *Isaiah 26:4*

Let us hold fast the confession of our hope without wavering, for He who promised is faithful... *Hebrews 10:23*

And by faith even Sarah, who was past childbearing age, was enabled to bear children because she considered Him faithful who had made the promise. *Hebrews 11:11*

It is a trustworthy statement: For if we died with him, we will also live with him; If we endure, we will also reign with him; If we deny him, he also will deny us; If we are faithless, he remains faithful, for he cannot deny himself. *2 Timothy 2:11-13*

Jesus answered and said to him, "If anyone loves me, he will keep my word; and my Father will love him, and we will come to him and make our abode with him. He who does not love me does not keep my words; and the word which you hear is not mine, but the Father's who sent me." *John 14:23-24*

If you keep my commandments, you will abide in my love; just as I have kept my Father's commandments and abide in His love. These things I have spoken to you so that my joy may be in you, and that your joy may be made full. This is my commandment, that you love one another, just as I have loved you. *John 15:10-12*

Let us hold fast the confession of our hope without wavering, for He who promised is faithful... *Hebrews 10:23*

For this is the love of God, that we keep His commandments; and His commandments are not burdensome. *1 John 5:3*

Retain the standard of sound words which you have heard from me, in the faith and love which are in Christ Jesus. Guard, through the Holy Spirit who dwells in us, the treasure which has been entrusted to you. *2 Timothy 1:13-14*

Do not let your heart be troubled; believe in God, believe also in me. *John 14:1*

Be on the alert, stand firm in the faith, act like men, be strong. *1 Corinthians 16:13*

And he said to him, "Well done, good servant; because you were faithful in a very little, have authority over ten cities." *Luke 19:17*

Father, if thou art willing, remove this cup from me; nevertheless not my will, but thine, be done. *Luke 22:42*

By one man's disobedience many were made sinners, so by one man's obedience many will be made righteous. *Romans 5:19*

We demolish arguments and every pretension that sets itself up against the knowledge of God, and we take captive every thought to make it obedient to Christ. *2 Corinthians 10:5*

In the days of his flesh, Jesus offered up prayers and supplications, with loud cries and tears, to him who was able to save him from death, and was heard for his godly fear. Although he was a Son, he learned obedience through what he suffered; and being made perfect he became the source of eternal salvation to all who obey him. *Hebrews 5:7-8*

These will wage war against the Lamb, and the Lamb will overcome them, because he is Lord of lords and King of kings, and those who are with him are the called and chosen and faithful. *Revelation 17:14*

Jesus showed us obedience and complete submission. Obedience is following an order when the circumstances allow, and complete submission is obeying even in impossible circumstances. Jesus taught the dutiful way of obedience and complete submission to the disbelieving people. By this he showed us the way to block Satan's basic nature and life elements. The satanic world incessantly tries to exploit and take advantage of human beings and the creation, but Jesus took the opposite direction. Jesus lived a life that Satan could not live—he was meek and humble, he practiced obedience and complete submission, and he lived a life of sacrifice and service. Because he lived with these qualities, Satan had to surrender. Jesus is the representative of all human beings. Likewise, unless you can live as Jesus taught in your daily life, being meek and humble, practicing obedience and complete submission, and ever sacrificing and serving others, know that you still belong to Satan's tribe. *Sun Myung Moon 10/27/1957*

Complete obedience means that a person has no sense of self in front of his subject partner. *Sun Myung Moon 8/23/1995*

Everyone should practice obedience. However, while anyone can obey, not everyone can totally surrender him or herself. Only through total surrender can we fulfill the indemnity condition. *Sun Myung Moon 6/7/1967*

Why does God require of us obedience? It is not to please God, but for us—for our joy. God puts us in the position of His ideal object partners and gives us responsibility to complete the purpose of re-creation. Therefore, we must push away and overcome the elements of the Fall. Because the Fall originated from disobedience, God commands us to have absolute obedience as the necessary condition to restore it. Therefore, in our religious way of life we should not complain. Nor should we make excuses. We must have absolute obedience. Absolute obedience requires hard work, but the purpose of that hard work is to set conditions that enable us to stand in the perfected position and achieve God's original goal of creation.

Therefore, if we sacrifice and work hard, we can enter the realm of perfection. We must go this way because there is no other way. Hence religion cannot emphasize enough the necessity of hard work, undertaken in faith. On the path of restoration, complaint is absolutely prohibited. The path of restoration is a tear-stained path of total sacrifice. Nevertheless, we should go joyfully and hopefully. It is the path of re-creation, which is hopeful for us, and we should rejoice in that hope. We are walking in faith, so we must not despair... *Sun Myung Moon 9/11/1972*

Throughout the long eons of history, God has been carrying out a providence to set up ways by which people, ignorant of the human portion of responsibility, could claim that they have fulfilled their portions of responsibility. This has always required absolute obedience. The original portion of responsibility was not fulfilled because Adam and Eve failed to obey God's commandment. Obeying God's Word is the first condition to complete the human portion of responsibility. For Adam and Eve, they could have completed their portion of responsibility by absolutely obeying God's command, "Do not eat of the fruit." Therefore, those seeking the way of restoration must absolutely obey God's words...That is what Jesus meant when he said, "He who loves father or mother more than me is not worthy of me; and he who loves son or daughter more than me is not worthy of me." *Sun Myung Moon 1/31/1986*

The measure of the life of faith is not money or any glory in this world...The center of infinite value is God alone; therefore, we should make God the standard of our life of faith. We should not pay attention to anything besides God. *Sun Myung Moon 7/29/1973*

Why did Adam fall? He fell because he lacked faith. Faithlessness was the first cause of the Fall... Consequently, we must go the way of faith. Through our faith, we should reverse the effects of our ancestors' fall due to their lack of faith. Then we can go upward. To go upward, even above the point where our ancestors fell, we must have absolute faith. *Sun Myung Moon 4/10/1983*

How serious are you, as you stand before God's tremendous Providence which He has been conducting through history? How much are you united with God's Will? Are you leading a life of absolute faith, centered on God's Will? You should be able to say, "Though winds and tempest blow, and though I may perish, my conviction is firm. I could be wrong, but God's Will can never be wrong." You should have such a rock-solid conviction. It is folly to desire for the Kingdom of God when your faith is ever changing from morning to evening. *Sun Myung Moon 7/25/1971*

To be healed, you need a doctor, the prescribed remedy, and a period of time. The doctor tells you, "Take this medicine for three days" or "I have to give you this medical treatment each day for a week." In the same way, a sin-sick person must keep faith in the Messiah, the Lord. He is your Physician. You must believe his word more than your own ideas. *Sun Myung Moon 10/14/1972*

CHAPTER 9

Christ came as the bridegroom, the true liberator of womankind

Jesus and the woman at the well

It was noontime when Jesus reached Samaria. Having walked since early morning from Judea, he was hot and weary when he sat by Jacob's well in the village of Sychar. Soon a Samaritan woman came to draw water, and Jesus said to her, "Please give me a drink." He was alone at the time because his disciples had gone into the village to buy some food. The woman was surprised, for Jews normally refuse to have anything to do with Samaritans. She said to Jesus, "You are a Jew, and I am a Samaritan woman. Why are you asking me for a drink?" Jesus replied, "If you only knew the gift God has for you and who you are speaking to, you would ask me, and I would give you living water." "But sir, you don't have a rope or a bucket," she said, "and this well is very deep. Where would you get this living water? And besides, do you think you're greater than our ancestor Jacob, who gave us this well? How can you offer better water than he and his sons and his animals enjoyed?"

Jesus replied, "Anyone who drinks this water will soon become thirsty again. But those who drink the water I give will never be thirsty again. It becomes a fresh, bubbling spring within them, giving them eternal life."

"Please, sir," the woman said, "give me this water! Then I'll never be thirsty again, and I won't have to come here to get water."

"Go and get your husband," Jesus told her.

"I don't have a husband," the woman replied.

Jesus said, "You're right! You don't have a husband—for you have had five husbands, and you aren't even married to the man you're living with now. You certainly spoke the truth!"

"Sir," the woman said, "you must be a prophet. So tell me, why is it that you Jews insist that Jerusalem is the only place of worship, while we Samaritans claim it is here at Mount Gerizim, where our ancestors worshiped?"

Jesus replied, "Believe me, dear woman, the time is coming when it will no longer matter whether you worship the Father on this mountain or in Jerusalem. You Samaritans know very little about the one you worship, while we Jews know all about Him, for salvation comes through the Jews. But the time is coming—indeed it's here now—when true worshipers will worship the Father in spirit and in truth. The Father is looking for those who will worship Him that way. For God is Spirit, so those who worship Him must worship in spirit and in truth."

The woman said, "I know the Messiah is coming—the one who is called Christ. When he comes, he will explain everything to us."

Then Jesus told her, "I am the Messiah!"

Just then his disciples came back. They were shocked to find him talking to a woman, but none of them had the nerve to ask, "What do you want with her?" or "Why are you talking to her?" The woman left her water jar beside the well and ran back to the village, telling everyone, "Come and see a man who told me everything I ever did! Could he possibly be the Messiah?" So the people came streaming from the village to see him. *John 4:1-30*

Commentary

Jesus' conversation with the Samaritan woman, recorded in the Gospel of John, is the longest recorded conversation between Jesus and another person. The conversation is remarkable because Jesus ignored the deep hostility existent between the two peoples. Jews despised Samaritans, because they believed Samaritans practiced a defective religion based on Judaism. The Savior also disregarded the customary social relations between men and women in ancient Israel. A Hebrew man did not talk with women in the street, not even with his mother, sister, daughter, or wife. A Hebrew man could divorce his wife if she was found talking in a familiar manner with another man.

But here was Jesus, on a hot summer day, shocking his

disciples by conversing with a woman from Samaria. By taking the time to speak with her, Jesus was conveying dignity and respect. Rather than viewing her through the lens of gender or social standing, Jesus saw the Samaritan woman as a person of value, an individual possessing her own relationship with God. His offer of salvation to this much-married woman was equivalent to the outreach he extended to the high-ranking Pharisees and Sadducees. Paul conveyed this same quality in *Galatians 3:28,* "There is neither Jew nor Gentile, neither slave nor free, nor is there male and female, for you are all one in Christ Jesus."

Jesus recognized the intrinsic value in all women, and they responded by being among his most ardent followers. Jesus' inner circle included Mary, her sister Martha, and Mary Magdalene. There were many women who travelled with the rabbi, following him from the shores of Galilee to the cross at Golgotha. This was an astonishing phenomenon, considering that in ancient Israel, women were not allowed to participate in synagogue worship and forbidden to enter the Temple beyond the Court of the Women.

The examples of speaking with the widow of Nain *(Luke 7:12-13),* healing the woman with the bleeding disorder *(Matthew 9:20-22),* or addressing the woman bent over for eighteen years *(Luke 13:10-13),* are but a few examples of the care and compassion he demonstrated towards those who were often treated as second-class citizens.

But Jesus is far more than a man who revolutionized

the treatment of women (and children) in ancient Israel. In order to understand the value of Christ to women, we need to look at the curse that came to Eve after the Fall in *Genesis 3:16*: "Your desire will be for your husband, and he will rule over you."

Why did the natural longing for a husband become a curse? It is because God was kicked out of His rightful position as Father of humankind by the fallen archangel Lucifer, who became Satan after having a carnal relationship with Eve. Eve transferred Lucifer's evil spiritual elements to Adam during the physical fall, thus preventing the first man from taking his position as a godly subject of love. In this manner, the devil infiltrated the line between man and God, thereby establishing a false dominion over humankind *(2 Corinthians 4:4)*. This usurpation has resulted in much suffering for women, the physically weaker and more vulnerable sex.

The secularization of the modern world has greatly contributed to women's misidentification of the source of their oppression. "Patriarchy" is a term commonly used by feminists to describe the mindset and social structure responsible for women's inequality. For Completed Testament Age (CTA) Christians,[42] however, the root of women's oppression is not connected to gender. It is connected, rather, to the thoughts and actions of those who place themselves in a superior position to God. CTA Christians believe that the story told in Genesis 3 is a symbolic account of an actual occurrence, and that restoring the relational dynamics within this story provides the key to female freedom.

When Eve chose to disobey God's commandment and unite with the false words of the rebellious archangel, she pierced the heart of God with an anguish still unbeknownst to almost all of humanity. True Father explained:

> The moment Adam and Eve fell, God's heart was torn so painfully He almost went insane. You should never forget about the Father who was shaken so thoroughly as to almost forget Himself. Have you ever thought about that? Even when fallen people on the earth watch their children die, they feel their bone marrow melt. They want to save their children even at the cost of their own lives. How must the heart of God been as He watched Adam and Eve walk the path toward the Fall and cross the line of death? Unless you understand that heart, there is no way for you to become God's sons and daughters.[43]

Eve willfully ignored God's wise counsel when she heeded Lucifer's temptation. Subsequently, the love she experienced with Adam was not in the realm of God's blessing. What was destined to be a glorious consummation instead became a premature act of fornication permeated with the rebellious spirit of Lucifer. Eve effectively spat in the face of God and His divine plan for her.

In loving Christ, then, women are able to reverse the

course of the Fall by obeying God instead of the archangel. By loving True Adam, the Son who did not succumb to fallen Eve, women can finally be restored to their proper positions as daughters of God. True liberation of women can only come from the love of Christ, a man completely free from fallen fervor. As men and women are reborn through the body and blood of Christ, they can pursue a relationship of pure, unstained love.

The nature of a true man seeks to love and safeguard his woman at the cost of his life. A godly woman is strong, yet she still wants to be protected and cherished by her man. A true husband will always have his wife's best interests at heart; he will never leave or betray her. The more the husband submits to Christ, the easier he makes it for his wife to follow him. Through unity with Christ, he is able to revoke the ancient curse of *Genesis 3:16*. By practicing the marital principles of love and respect as described in *Ephesians 5:33*, the love of Christ will be increasingly infused into a couple's marriage.

Christ is called the Bridegroom throughout the Scriptures; Paul tells us in *2 Corinthians 11:2*, "For I am jealous for you with a godly jealousy; for I betrothed you to one husband, so that to Christ I might present you as a pure virgin."

True Father continually urged his followers to draw close to Jesus throughout his ministry:

> Christians know that Jesus is Lord and that he is the
> source of love. They want to unite with him and receive

that love. But they cannot do so by simply reading the Bible. It is only when they yearn and long for Jesus that they can become a part of him. If they are truly close to Jesus, then when he feels sad, they feel sad. The emotions or feelings of a man do have an influence upon the seed in his flesh. When a man feels happy, that feeling of happiness affects his own seed. Likewise, when he feels sad, that feeling of sadness affects his seed. Then what does it really mean to believe in Jesus? Jesus is a man. He was like the original Adam before the fall. So after all, Jesus is the spiritual father. Without uniting with your father, you cannot be reborn. Christianity is the only religion that teaches people to long for Jesus and love him and welcome him as a bride welcomes her bridegroom. We should want to penetrate Jesus even to the marrow of his bone...How many people have faith to the extent that they actually want to go into the flesh and body of Jesus? You cannot enter the body of Jesus except through heart and love...[44]

It is love, in the end, that will liberate all of us. Women's liberation will finally be achieved when we women realize that true freedom begins and ends with Christ as the Bridegroom of our soul. Eve is not to be venerated or worshiped. She is loved, restored, and fulfilled through a relationship with her King of Kings.

Scripture

I will rejoice greatly in the Lord,
My soul will exult in my God;
For He has clothed me with garments of salvation,
He has wrapped me with a robe of righteousness,
As a bridegroom decks himself with a garland,
And as a bride adorns herself with her jewels. *Isaiah 61:10*

You are all fair, my love,
And there is no spot in you.
Come with me from Lebanon, my spouse,
With me from Lebanon.
Look from the top of Amana,
From the top of Senir and Hermon,
From the lions' dens,
From the mountains of the leopards.
You have ravished my heart,
My sister, my spouse;
You have ravished my heart
With one look of your eyes,
With one link of your necklace.
How fair is your love,
My sister, my spouse!
How much better than wine is your love,
And the scent of your perfumes
Than all spices!

Your lips, O my spouse,
Drip as the honeycomb;
Honey and milk are under your tongue;
And the fragrance of your garments
Is like the fragrance of Lebanon.
A garden enclosed
Is my sister, my spouse,
A spring shut up,
A fountain sealed. *Song of Solomon 4:7-12*

The Lord is good,
a stronghold in the day of trouble;
He knows those who take refuge in Him. *Nahum 1:7*

Then the disciples of John came to him, asking, "Why do we and the Pharisees fast, but Your disciples do not fast?" And Jesus said to them, "The attendants of the bridegroom cannot mourn as long as the bridegroom is with them, can they? But the days will come when the bridegroom is taken away from them, and then they will fast." *Matthew 9:14-15*

Then the kingdom of heaven will be comparable to ten virgins, who took their lamps and went out to meet the bridegroom. Five of them were foolish, and five were prudent. For when the foolish took their lamps, they took no oil with them, but the prudent took oil in flasks along with their lamps. Now while the bridegroom was delaying, they all got drowsy and began to sleep. But at midnight there was a shout, "Behold, the bridegroom! Come out to meet him." Then all those virgins rose and trimmed their lamps. The foolish said to the prudent, "Give us some of your oil, for our lamps are going out." But the prudent answered, "No, there will not be enough for us and you too; go instead to the dealers and buy some for yourselves." And while they were going away to make the purchase, the bridegroom came, and those who were ready went in with him to the wedding feast; and the door was shut. *Matthew 25:1-10*

He who has the bride is the bridegroom; but the friend of the bridegroom, who stands and hears him rejoices greatly because of the bridegroom's voice So this joy of mine has been made full. *John 3:29*

Be imitators of me, as I am of Christ. Now I commend you because you remember me in everything and maintain the traditions even as I delivered them to you. But I want you to understand that the head of every man is Christ, the head of a wife is her husband, and the head of Christ is God. *1 Corinthians 11:1-3*

Nevertheless let each one of you in particular so love his own wife as himself, and let the wife see that she respects her husband. *Ephesians 5:33*

Let us rejoice and be glad and give the glory to Him, for the marriage of the Lamb has come and His bride has made herself ready. *Revelation 19:7*

And I saw the holy city, new Jerusalem, coming down out of heaven from God, made ready as a bride adorned for her husband. *Revelation 21:2*

The Spirit and the bride say, "Come." And let the one who hears say, "Come." And let the one who is thirsty come; let the one who wishes take the water of life without cost. *Revelation 22:17*

What did Jesus, who crossed the path of crucifixion to come seeking us, leave behind? He left the mission of the bride and bridegroom. Accordingly, now the Lord will appear as the bridegroom in your prayers. You are the bride and the Lord is the bridegroom, and this is the appearance with which he will come before you. When you meet the Lord who comes as the bridegroom, you have to always think about the recompense of the blood shed on the cross.

What did Jesus, who came seeking us, leave behind for us of this day? What is that which he has given us, having found us through his doleful life of suffering and death on the cross? Jesus left behind for us the light of life. He risked his life and came looking for us, and the gift that he brought was the light that lit up this dark world. There-fore, when we shed tears of gratitude while reflecting on the death of Jesus, we will come to understand his heart and his situation.

What is the next thing that Jesus left for us? He left be-hind water and oil. He left behind water and oil with which he can heal our wounds as we undergo tremen-dous ordeals and many wounds are inflicted on us. Ac-cordingly, we must use the light Jesus provided for us to discover our wounds and wash them with the water and oil. Knowing our sins and realizing that we are na-ked, we must weave a holy gown and wear it. Such a time has come. Similarly, only after you have lit up your heart and mind to wash all the sins away, healed the wounds, and worn the gown, can you realize today the dream of Jesus who passed away two thousand years ago. Now, we must light up the lantern in our hearts, wash our bodies with the water, and apply the oil to our wounds. Finally, after wearing the gown granted to us, we should bear the cross so that Jesus does not have to and bow before Jesus. This is the task man on the earth must fulfill. Do not wish for Jesus to bear the cross for you, but bear it yourself. It is not Jesus who should bear it; you must become the peo-ple who give out the light of life. Then being equipped with all the power, wear the gown that can represent the light of the eternal and unchanging value. After that, go over the cross to become the beloved brides who will hold onto Jesus and bow before him, saying, "Lord, please rest in peace eternally." God is hoping these kinds of brides will appear. *Sun Myung Moon 5/20/1956*

Hence, the ultimate mission Jesus left behind for us is contained in the words, "You are my bride." At that time, Jesus could not speak directly, even to his beloved disciples. Instead, he spoke from the position of making a promise for the future. You have to understand this heart of Jesus. Centering on the will that Heaven entrusted to him, Jesus' heart of love toward his disciples, the Israelites and Judaism remained unchanged. However, because they were ignorant people, an ignorant religious group and ignorant disciples, Jesus alone took on all the arrows as the spearhead in the conflict with Satan. To pioneer a path for their survival, he walked a course of ordeals. In other words, you have to clearly understand that Jesus was a sorrowful person who did not live in an environment in which he could frankly reveal the heart deep inside his mind, the ideology of the bride and bridegroom of Heaven.

As Jesus was leaving, he spoke the words to us on the earth, "You are my bride" as the target of hope that could usher in the new day of joy. Yet what happened to that ideology of the bride? Until now, there has been no one who, during the course of thousands of years of history, won the victory in the bitter conflict with Satan and stood in the position of Jesus' bride. Accordingly, you today must establish the ideology of the bride which was not established by the chosen people of Israel and the beloved disciples 2,000 years ago. You must learn to deal with the heart of Jesus on your own accord.

From what position did Jesus speak his words? His words were left behind to help the people, who believed in him as the bridegroom, develop the real qualifications of a bride and be connected to his heartbreaking situation. Therefore, we today must fulfill the real meaning of the words Jesus gave us. We must rectify the words of the bridegroom by becoming the bride Jesus wants, and reach the position where we can experience the internal heart that Jesus felt. You have to understand that if no one reaches this state, then the purpose of the words Jesus spoke throughout his thirty years of life cannot be fulfilled. *Sun Myung Moon 10/4/1957*

God is your Father and you are your Father's daughters. How much God has longed to embrace His daughters in His bosom? For that reason, you should become God's filial daughters... If each of you becomes a filial daughter, all your family members will follow suit. By the same token, the entire nation, world and cosmos will unite with you. You will become God's number one victorious daughter, a saint to the world, a holy daughter to the cosmos. That is how you become a mistress in the realm of the royal family. *Sun Myung Moon 5/26/1998*

The grandmother, mother, one's wife, and wife of one's son are all like young widows and they are waiting for the groom. But the groom has no nation with which he can take possession of the world! Who is the groom? It is Reverend Moon. I had made compromises with Heaven, pledged, and decided the method to be able to handle the providence even without having a nation, and so you can't help but follow my will at all costs. One must resemble by uniting with God's blood lineage and tradition. Children must be born resembling their parents through the same tradition and blood lineage. Anyone who doesn't resemble their parents is false. *Sun Myung Moon 5/21/2012*

Women are Eve; they cannot decide on their own paths to follow. You want to keep my photograph and live day and night before me. You don't want to go somewhere else and get married. Even after one hundred years, when you are in the spirit world, you can call out "Father" and we can meet and discuss things and understand each other fully in the same way that I am able to communicate with heaven. Do you think you will not be able to communicate this way? I am trying to liberate you. *Sun Myung Moon 7/7/2009*

Husbands, the woman standing before you is God's daughter. Also, before she is your wife, she is humanity's daughter. If you can love her as God's beloved daughter and a woman whom all humanity loves, then you are qualified to be her husband. Men who do not respect their wives are not true husbands. Do you have such regard for your wife? If not, you should change, even now. Wives, you should not think that your husband only belongs to you. First, he is a son of God; next, he represents all the men in the world. You should become a woman who can love this man more than all humanity can, and love him more than God loves him. *Sun Myung Moon 10/3/1976*

Since your goal is to come as close as possible to God, then you need to deeply long to be with me. *Sun Myung Moon 4/1/1977*

CHAPTER 10

Christ is the Judge
who rules with God's authority

The amazing authority of Jesus

They went to Capernaum; and when the Sabbath came, he entered the synagogue and taught. They were astounded at his teaching, for he taught them as one having authority, and not as the scribes. Just then there was in their synagogue a man with an unclean spirit, and he cried out, "What have you to do with us, Jesus of Nazareth? Have you come to destroy us? I know who you are, the Holy One of God." But Jesus rebuked him, saying, "Be silent, and come out of him!" And the unclean spirit, convulsing him and crying with a loud voice, came out of him. They were all amazed, and they kept on asking one another, "What is this? A new teaching—with authority! He commands even the unclean spirits, and they obey him." At once his fame began to spread throughout the surrounding region of Galilee. *Mark 1:21-28*

Triumph over the enemy

Jesus, full of the Holy Spirit, left the Jordan and was led by the Spirit into the wilderness, where for forty days he was tempted by the devil. He ate nothing during those days, and at the end of them he was hungry. The devil said to him, "If you are the Son of God, tell this stone to become bread." Jesus answered, "It is written: 'Man shall not live on bread alone.' "

The devil led him up to a high place and showed him in an instant all the kingdoms of the world. And he said to him, "I will give you all their authority and splendor; it has been given to me, and I can give it to anyone I want to. If you worship me, it will all be yours."

Jesus answered, "It is written: 'Worship the Lord your God and serve Him only.' "

The devil led him to Jerusalem and had him stand on the highest point of the temple. "If you are the Son of God," he said, "throw yourself down from here. For it is written: 'He will command His angels concerning you to guard you carefully; they will lift you up in their hands, so that you will not strike your foot against a stone.' "

Jesus answered, "It is said: 'Do not put the Lord your God to the test.' " *Luke 4:1-12*

Jesus clears the Temple

In the temple courts he found men selling cattle, sheep, and doves, and money changers seated at their tables. So he made a whip out of cords and drove all from the temple courts, both sheep and cattle. He poured out the coins of the money changers and overturned their tables. To those selling doves He said, "Get these out of here! How dare you turn My Father's house into a marketplace!" *John 2:14-16*

True Father's victorious return

In a country where people are executed for owning a Bible, Reverend Moon fearlessly proclaimed the gospel. Once the center of Christianity in northeast Asia, North Korea became staunchly atheistic under the iron-fisted rule of Kim Il Sung beginning in the mid-twentieth century. Nevertheless, in November 1991, True Father flew to North Korea with a small entourage to meet with the same government that had imprisoned him decades earlier for preaching God's Word. Bo Hi Pak, who accompanied him on his visit, recalls the speech True Father gave to executive officials of the North Korean Worker's Party. Facing possible death, True Father spoke boldly, imbued with Heaven's authority. Pak recalls his shock when Father took charge at a conference room meeting with Kim Il Sung's top leaders:

> But then it happened. Reverend Moon, who was sitting next to me, stood up all of a sudden. Both our group and the North Koreans were somewhat startled, wondering what was going on; this was the point where the morning session of our discussions was to have finished. So why was Reverend Moon standing up like this?

Reverend Moon spoke. "At this point, I'd better say a few words. Could I have a glass of water, please," he said. He drank the whole glass of water. Mr. Yoon (the Committee Chairman) visibly startled, said, "Reverend Moon, wouldn't you prefer to speak sitting down?" to which he replied, "No. What I have to say is important, so I'd better stand while I say it." And then he began to speak. Seeing the intensity with which Reverend Moon started, long years of experience told me intuitively what he was going to say. The reason he got up from his seat indicated the content; he got up so that he could move his body about freely while speaking. I tensed up. I had no idea how things were going to unfold. Reverend Moon began to summarize the Unification Principle.

First of all he asked the North Koreans if they knew what the purpose of God's Creation was and proceeded to explain human history, starting with the first human ancestors, Adam and Eve. His speech comprised all the core elements of the Unification Principle: the ideal of God's creation, the Fall of Adam and Eve, the history of God's efforts for human salvation, the mission of Jesus Christ, and the ideology of returning resurrection and the ideology of True Parents.

As he continued his explanation, Reverend Moon's fervor steadily increased. He had apparently forgotten that we were in North Korea, in the Mahn Soo Dae Assembly Halls. The only thing he was focused on was pouring out, directly and clearly, the words that God was giving him...Reverend Moon was giving an historical sermon to the core ranks of the Democratic People's Republic of Korea. For Mr. Yoon, as well as for all the officials from the government and the North Korean Worker's Party who were present, it was the first time in their lives to hear a sermon, to listen to the word of God.

For the moment, everything was all right. Presently, however, with perspiration pouring out, Reverend Moon was roaring away as if he were speaking before a huge audience at a rally. He treated the North Korean officials gathered there not like hosts, but like members of the Unification Church.

Reverend Moon spoke while jabbing his finger, pointing it at Chairman Yoon. "What's all this about 'the Juche ideology'? You're telling me the Juche ideology is an ideology centered on humans? How the heck can human beings be the center of the universe? Don't you know that human beings are just another kind of created being? Human beings are not the Creator! They aren't! Have you got that, Chairman Yoon? They're created beings, created, I tell you! So, above human beings, you have God. God exists on a higher level than human beings! But you don't even know that, and you talk all this rubbish about the wonderful Juche ideology. And you're saying that we can achieve unification through the Juche ideology? Not a chance! Not a chance in a million! I'm telling you that you have to attend God, you have to pay more attention to God than you do to Juche ideology. The only way for North Korea to survive is for you to connect with God and bring Him here! Hey! Chairman Yoon! Do you get it? I'm asking you if you get it! Why don't you answer?... There is no way you can bring national unification with the Juche ideology! Unification is something that God will achieve. That's why you can't achieve Korean unification without going through Godism and head-wing thought! No way! National unification is going to be brought about by me! I'm the one who'll do it! You should entrust the problem of national unification to me, you hear! I will rescue North Korea. Have you got it, Chairman Yoon?... You should entrust North Korea to me. Let me take care of it for three years. A good living standard will be available to everyone. I don't mean I want to be president. What I'm saying is that I'll open the way for everyone to live well under President Kim Il Sung."

Again, we all held our breath in suspense. If Reverend Moon continued to make Kim Il Sung the subject of his discussion, something was bound to happen.

"Don't get me wrong; I like President Kim. But even that fellow has to listen to what I have to say. My words! Get it, Mr. Chairman?"

Again Reverend Moon poked his finger at Mr. Yoon. "Why don't you answer me, huh?" He was treating Chairman Yoon like an elementary school student. And the one receiving this treatment was one of the highest officials in the North Korean Worker's Party.

As soon as our car started off, the committee member let his anger explode. "How on earth can you behave like that when you come here as guests? We can't forgive that sort of thing. In this country, that's enough to get you the death penalty. If the citizens of Pyongyang heard what was said, they'd come here with big sticks and beat the daylights out of you all." He was so indignant that drops of spit came from his mouth as he berated us.

I desperately tried to placate him. "Please calm down, Mr. Vice Chairman. Reverend Moon only said the things he did out of love for this nation, for this people. There are lots of different ways of expressing love, don't you think? Why would Reverend Moon go so far as to say those things? He was simply being straightforward."

At the luncheon table, it was just our small group from the Unification movement.

"I just said what I had to say, didn't I?" Reverend Moon said. "Do you think I went a little bit too far?" He flashed a big smile.

"Father," I quietly answered. "I think you had better forget about meeting Kim Il Sung."

To this, Reverend Moon's words fell like a lightning

bolt. "Did I come here just to meet Kim Il Sung? I tell you, I came here to speak the truth. God wants me to say everything I have to say at least once before I have to leave..."[45] *Bo Hi Pak*

Commentary

Jesus manifested his role as God's Judge throughout his life. Whether casting out demons, subjugating Satan in the wilderness, or whipping covetous priests in the Temple, Christ demonstrated an authoritative strength that transcended earthly power.

As a being of absolute goodness, Jesus bore his role as Adjudicator with unshakeable confidence. Originally, God intended to "take residence" in Adam, and reign through His Son in both the physical and spiritual realms as the eternal King of Kings. This would have included the role of Judge, for God is the ultimate arbiter of good and evil.

Because of the Fall, however, the first man was adopted into Satan's lineage, preventing God from establishing a True Adamic presence in either the physical or spirit world. For God to fulfill His role as Sovereign Lord of humankind, Christ must return as the Last Adam *(1 Corinthians 15:45)*.

Jesus was born as True Adam, and was the image of the invisible God, the firstborn over all creation. The fullness of God lived in his bodily form *(Colossians 2:9)*. Because he was one with the Father, there was no condition for Satan in any way to influence his spirit. Jesus is the all-wise God in the flesh and was appointed by the Father to be our Judge *(John 5:27, Acts 10:42)*.

It was Jesus' custom to go to synagogue on the Sabbath. Synagogues, widely scattered throughout Israel, were devoted to the study of Scripture. The scribes who led the study were trusted scholars considered to be the authorities on the Torah within the local community. The best seats in the synagogue were reserved for them; people rose to their feet when the learned men entered a room.

Unlike the scribes, however, Jesus taught with an authority that emanated from his personal being. His commanding presence did not come from his credentials or his reputation, but by the fact that he was the substantial embodiment of God's Word and all Scripture pointed to him. Mark did not record the content of Jesus' preaching in *Mark 1:21-22*; he simply wrote that people were amazed by the potency of Christ's words. Jesus's subsequent rebuke of the demonic spirit in *Mark 1:23-26* demonstrated that his arbitration originated from a powerfully divine source.

The boldness with which Jesus spoke came from the core of his being; every cell of his body was filled with the love and truth of God. Even after 40 days of fasting, he had the power to exhort the devil with holy righteousness. Jesus chastised Satan for his false claims as ruler, and treated him as the servant of God he was created to be.

When Jesus unleashed his handmade whip onto the

money-changers, he was making it clear that his Father's house was not to be defiled. He sought no earthly permission when he scattered the money and overturned tables. He didn't register with the Sanhedrin and ask, "What's the protocol for cleansing the Temple?" He didn't seek approval from anybody except the Father. And he knew that his Father disapproved of the corrupt pecuniary practices taking place in the Temple.

Jesus was a fair judge who never discriminated or showed special favor. True Father explained that to be fair, you must have a clear, even conscience. An unbiased judge should have no prejudices on the horizontal level. When that clear conscience is evident, then, "...the heart of God or the Spirit of God will work in a vertical way, and a ninety- degree angle is made. If the conscience is not even, the angle formed is not ninety degrees, and you will receive the wrong message...If the ninety-degree angle is maintained, when you face a problem you immediately know whether it is good or bad. The reflection is very accurate..."[46] Only in this manner can a judge be an impartial decision-maker in the pursuit of justice.

It was with a complete "evenness of mind" that True Father met and spoke with the communist leaders of North Korea. Like Jesus, True Father spoke uncomfortable truth at the risk of his life. When he stood to address the military men seated at the Mahn Soo Dae Assembly Hall, he exercised his role as God's Judge by pronouncing atheistic

"Juche" to be a false ideology.

Astonishingly, Kim Il Sung ordered that Reverend Moon's speech, filled with references of God, be published in North Korea's only newspaper, *Rodong Shinmun*. To everyone's amazement, the complete text of his "sermon" appeared the following day in the paper for all citizens to read.[47]

Judgment is unpleasant to think about when we are the ones being judged—but the truth is, we were all created to desire justice. We intuitively know that good and evil exist, and we long for evil to be vanquished in order for goodness to reign. In a world of relativism, the lines between criminality and innocence become fuzzy and indistinct. Christ, the embodiment of the absolute goodness of God, is desperately needed by humankind as the ultimate, objective mediator of justice.

Jesus did not hesitate to take a subjective stance towards the Sadducees and Pharisees, the religious and political leaders of his time. Although they possessed worldly power through their external prestige, status, and connections with Rome, Jesus judged them for their flagrant ungodliness. Whether facing evil spirits, corrupt priests, or the devil himself, Jesus never shirked his responsibility to separate good from evil in the world around him.

Despite the increased risk to his personal safety, Reverend Moon spearheaded the ideological dismantling of communist thought through the creation of CAUSA[48] International. Formed in the 1980s, CAUSA was dedicated to exposing the pseudo-scientific nature of Marxist-Leninism. CAUSA lecturers emphasized the central point that communism will never accomplish its goal of human equality, because Marxist ideology is based on the assumption that there is no God. Reverend Moon developed a worldview called "Godism," a logical counterproposal to Marxism which asserted that true equality can only be achieved by affirming God's existence. In this manner, Reverend Moon fulfilled his messianic role as Judge by exposing and ruling against satanic atheistic ideology *(Ecclesiastes 12:14)*. By using the Rod of Iron,[49] the Word of God *(Isaiah 11:4, Revelation 19:15)*, he enabled the people of the world to separate from the evil ideology of communism.

Because of our inherently sinful nature, we submit to Christ in order to be under God's authority. This submission is not based on power, but on love. We surrender because we know that Christ is blameless before God, yet loves us sinners unconditionally. We know that his truth will set us free. We can trust him to be our Judge, for he will only speak and act as directed by the Father.

Jesus' and True Father's love and attendance to God is different from ours. There is a total oneness of mind, heart, and will between them and Heavenly Father. They alone have the power to claim this world back from Satan because there is no trace of evil within them. They have completely defeated the devil and stand as True Judge, True Bridegroom, and True King of this world.

Scripture

For he is coming, for he is coming to judge the earth.
He shall judge the world with righteousness,
And the peoples with his truth. *Psalm 96:13*

....

The Lord says to my Lord: "Sit at My right hand until I make your enemies a footstool for your feet." *Psalm 110:1*

....

"Behold, the days are coming," says the Lord,
"That I will raise to David a Branch of righteousness;
A King shall reign and prosper,
And execute judgment and righteousness in the earth.
In His days Judah will be saved,
And Israel will dwell safely;
Now this is His name by which He will be called:
The Lord Our righteousness." *Jeremiah 23:5-6*

....

Then speak to him, saying, Thus says the Lord of hosts, saying:
"Behold, the Man whose name is the Branch!
From His place He shall branch out,
And He shall build the temple of the Lord;
Yes, He shall build the temple of the Lord
He shall bear the glory,
And shall sit and rule on His throne;
So He shall be a priest on His throne,

And the counsel of peace shall be between them both."
Zechariah 6:12-13

Not everyone who says to me, "Lord, Lord," will enter the kingdom of heaven, but only the one who does the will of my Father who is in heaven. Many will say to me on that day, "Lord, Lord, did we not prophesy in your name and in your name drive out demons and in your name perform many miracles?" Then I will tell them plainly, "I never knew you. Away from me, you evildoers!"
Therefore everyone who hears these words of mine and puts them into practice is like a wise man who built his house on the rock. The rain came down, the streams rose, and the winds blew and beat against that house; yet it did not fall, because it had its foundation on the rock. But everyone who hears these words of mine and does not put them into practice is like a foolish man who built his house on sand. The rain came down, the streams rose, and the winds blew and beat against that house, and it fell with a great crash.
When Jesus had finished saying these things, the crowds were amazed at his teaching, because he taught as one who had authority, and not as their teachers of the law.
Matthew 7:21-29

Knowing their thoughts, Jesus said, "Why do you entertain evil thoughts in your hearts? Which is easier: to say,

'Your sins are forgiven,' or to say, 'Get up and walk'? But I want you to know that the Son of Man has authority on earth to forgive sins." So he said to the paralyzed man, "Get up, take your mat and go home." Then the man got up and went home. When the crowd saw this, they were filled with awe; and they praised God, who had given such authority to man. *Matthew 9:4-8*

When the Son of Man comes in his glory and all his angels are with him, he will sit on his glorious throne. The people of every nation will be gathered in front of him. He will separate them as a shepherd separates the sheep from the goats. He will put the sheep on his right but the goats on his left. *Matthew 25:31-33*

All authority has been given to me in heaven and on earth. *Matthew 28:18*

And as he spoke, a certain Pharisee asked Him to dine with him. So he went in and sat down to eat. When the Pharisee saw it, he marveled that he had not first washed before dinner.

Then the Lord said to him, "Now you Pharisees make the outside of the cup and dish clean, but your inward part is full of greed and wickedness. Foolish ones! Did not he who made the outside make the inside also? But rather give alms of such things as you have; then indeed all things are clean to you.

But woe to you Pharisees! For you tithe mint and rue and all manner of herbs, and pass by justice and the love of God. These you ought to have done, without leaving the others undone. Woe to you Pharisees! For you love the best seats in the synagogues and greetings in the market-places. Woe to you, scribes and Pharisees, hypocrites! For you are like graves which are not seen, and the men who walk over them are not aware of them."

Then one of the lawyers answered and said to him, "Teach-er, by saying these things you reproach us also."

And he said, "Woe to you also, lawyers! For you load men with burdens hard to bear, and you yourselves do not touch the burdens with one of your fingers. Woe to you! For you build the tombs of the prophets, and your fathers killed them. In fact, you bear witness that you approve the deeds of your fathers; for they indeed killed them, and you build their tombs. Therefore the wisdom of God also said, I will send them prophets and apostles, and some of them they will kill and persecute, that the blood of all the prophets which was shed from the foundation of the world may be required of this generation, from the blood of Abel to the blood of Zechariah who perished between the altar and the temple. Yes, I say to you, it shall be required of this generation. Woe to you lawyers! For you have taken away the key of knowledge. You did not enter in yourselves, and those who were entering in you hindered." *Luke 11:37-52*

The seventy-two returned with joy and said, "Lord, even the demons submit to us in your name." *Luke 10:16-17*

Yet to all who did receive him, to those who believed in his name, he gave the right to become children of God. *John 1:12*

For I have not spoken on my own authority; but the Father who sent me gave me a command, what I should say and what I should speak. *John 12:49*

After Jesus said this, he looked toward heaven and prayed, "Father, the hour has come. Glorify your son, that your Son may glorify you. For you granted him authority over all people that he might give eternal life to all those you have given him." *John 17:1-2*

He commanded us to preach to the people [both Jew and Gentile], and to solemnly testify that He is the One who has been appointed and ordained by God as Judge of the living and the dead. *Acts 10:42*

For we must all appear before the judgment seat of Christ, so that each one may be recompensed for his deeds in the body, according to what he has done, whether good or bad. *2 Corinthians 5:10*

In the past God overlooked such ignorance, but now he commands all people everywhere to repent. For he has set a day when he will judge the world with justice by the man he has appointed. He has given proof of this to everyone by raising him from the dead. *Acts 17:30-31*

For not even the Father judges anyone, but He has given all judgment to the Son. *John 5:22*

I can do nothing on My own initiative. As I hear, I judge; and My judgment is just, because I do not seek My own will, but the will of Him who sent Me. *John 5:30*

I have many things to speak and to judge concerning you, but He who sent Me is true; and the things which I heard from Him, these I speak to the world. *John 8:26*

And Jesus said, "For judgment I came into this world, so that those who do not see may see, and that those who see may become blind." *John 9:39*

This will take place on the day when God judges people's secrets through Jesus Christ, as my gospel declares. *Romans 2:16*

And I saw heaven opened, and behold, a white horse, and He who sat on it is called Faithful and True, and in righteousness He judges and wages war. *Revelation 19:11*

Jesus was indignant and used strong language, calling the Jewish leaders a brood of vipers. He was justified in saying that because they were just thinking about themselves and their own denominations. It was the same kind of thinking as Satan's, for they shared the same blood. To be truly religious, the Jews should have been thinking about the world and God and not so much about their own religion; they should have had stronger love for God and mankind and all things. If all of you are not that way but think about yourself and your own denomination more than the world, then certainly you are a brood of vipers. That's why Jesus spoke to the Jews the way he did. *Sun Myung Moon 4/1/1978*

The purpose of judgment is not to capture men but to capture the enemy. It seeks not to liberate all things, but to liberate men. *Sun Myung Moon, The Way of God's Will*

We should be like God's shadow. Only when we become completely one with God as His object partner, like His shadow, can we lead others in any situation. Only then can we lift our heads and speak with authority. *Sun Myung Moon 11/13/1992*

We are transcending Satan's limited realm. Once that work is completed, God can take dominion over the universe without any difficulty. Then, Satan's realm will be gone

from the earth, and the new sovereignty of Heaven will arrive. With God on high, Satan will disappear and Heaven's new sovereignty will be established. God's dominion will extend from individuals to the cosmos, and God will reign for the first time in human history. The time is at hand when all-transcendent, all-encompassing, all-sovereign and almighty God can do all that He desires. Being all encompassing, God will reign over the entire world that formerly had been in Satan's possession. Being almighty, God will do whatever He pleases, holding all authority over Satan.
Sun Myung Moon 9/8/1998

Since Christ will be born on the earth at his Second Advent, it is written: "She brought forth a male child, one who is to rule all the nations with a rod of iron, but her child was caught up to God and to his throne." The rod of iron here signifies the Word of God, with which the Lord will judge the sinful world and restore the Kingdom of Heaven on earth. It was earlier explained in detail that judgment by fire is judgment by the Word. Hence, the Word of Jesus, which will be our judge on the Last Day, is the same Word by which heaven and earth will be cast into the fire of judgment, and is the very breath of the Lord's mouth by which he will slay the lawless one. The Word Jesus speaks is also called "the breath of his lips" and "the rod of his mouth." It is symbolized by the rod of iron, as it is written, "He shall rule them with a rod of iron, as when earthen pots are broken in pieces."

The verse speaks of a male child, who is born of a woman and is caught up to God and to His throne. Who, then, is born of a woman as someone worthy to sit on God's throne and rule all the nations with the Word of God? He can be none other than Christ at the Second Advent, who will be born on the earth with a new name known only to himself. He will rule as the King of Kings and build the Kingdom of Heaven. *Exposition of Divine Principle, p.390*

I am merciless towards evil, but simply bow down to good. *Sun Myung Moon 2/13/2011*

Even though there are millions of people in the entire universe, only the person who can serve the One Being can become the leader of the human world. No one, however, knows about the One Being, God. *Sun Myung Moon 2/28/2010*

The Lord and Savior is coming! What will the Lord do when he comes? He is to rule the nation and the world. Will he rule arbitrarily, governing any way he pleases? No, he will rule with truth. Wherever in the world the Lord travels, he will govern with truth. *Sun Myung Moon 6/15/1969*

Final judgment is based on a single, simple formula: whether or not a person is motivated by selfish or unselfish desires. *Sun Myung Moon 10/3/1976*

Wherever a law is needed judgment becomes necessary. Basically, judgment is always given according to the degree of selfishness of an act. *Sun Myung Moon 6/12/1977*

There is always a test to pass at each level before you can advance further. Who is testing you? It is not God but Satan and the satanic world who will test you. Satan is in the position of prosecutor while God is in the position of judge and you are the defendant. Jesus Christ is your lawyer. There is a court of judgment on every level of your advancement and finally God, the universal sovereign, has His own court. No one can escape from defending himself there...

My conscience is clear in the sight of God. I can stride boldly forward to meet God without shame. When I go to spirit world I am indeed an attorney for the defense of suffering humanity. I have the power to truly prosecute the prosecutor, Satan. The day will come when we can all prosecute Satan, revealing his crimes and commanding that he not bother mankind anymore. That will be your day of victory. *Sun Myung Moon 11/21/1976*

Christianity prospered for two thousand years, but in the two decades since 1960 it began a steep decline. I want to clearly declare that the reason for that decline is the Christian opposition of the new sovereignty, the new power and truth of God. If the Christian cultural sphere continues such a trend then it will be caught in an unavoidable decline.

On the other hand, if Christianity will accept me and repent, and if America will accept me and repent, then there is a ray of hope. There is no other way for either America or Christianity to find hope. Many people think this declaration is boastful and blasphemous, but I have declared this with the authority of the entire spirit world, which already supports it. I merely bear testimony to the truth. *Sun Myung Moon 4/18/1978*

There are people who claim that there is no such thing as God, that they can be a god and mold this world as they desire. Although they want to become God themselves, in reality they are colliding with the true universal plus. Such people become the worst kind of dictators. *Sun Myung Moon 2/13/1977*

Have we only regarded God as a concept? Have we only honored Him as Lord in worship? That is not right. God is the Lord of our life, the Ruler of our daily affairs and the Subject of our thought. *Sun Myung Moon 2/12/1961*

In the Last Days, judgment by the saints precedes judgment by God and Jesus *(1 Corinthians 6:2)*. Therefore, the testimonies by the saints are important, and you should have three persons who can testify to you. The content of their testimony will be decided by how deeply you have shared sorrow, pain and joy with them. *Sun Myung Moon, The Way of God's Will*

CHAPTER 11

Christ is the King of Kings who will usher in the Kingdom of Heaven on Earth

Jesus teaches us to pray for the Kingdom to come

And when you pray, you shall not be like the hypocrites. For they love to pray standing in the synagogues and on the corners of the streets, that they may be seen by men. Assuredly, I say to you, they have their reward. But you, when you pray, go into your room, and when you have shut your door, pray to your Father who is in the secret place; and your Father who sees in secret will reward you openly. And when you pray, do not use vain repetitions as the heathen do. For they think that they will be heard for their many words. Therefore do not be like them. For your Father knows the things you have need of before you ask Him. In this manner, therefore, pray:

Our Father who art in heaven,
hallowed be thy name.
Thy kingdom come.
Thy will be done
On earth as it is in heaven.
Give us this day our daily bread.

And forgive us our debts,
As we forgive our debtors.
And lead us not into temptation,
But deliver us from the evil.
Matthew 6:5-13

God's nation is the Kingdom

The day had finally arrived, February 21, 1980. It was True Father's sixtieth birthday. All New York City Performing Arts members had been working hard in preparation for this day. We felt truly blessed to have been selected to restore the Grand Ballroom of the New Yorker Hotel. The Grand Ballroom was on the Mezzanine floor of the hotel which had been purchased by HSA-UWC[50] in 1976. It was the venue where Father gave many Holy Day speeches; it was also the room where he had introduced me to my future husband nine months earlier.

The Performing Arts Department had been separated into two teams to support the restoration effort: the group responsible for the actual remodeling, and the group designated to raise funds for the project. I had participated as a fundraiser, and was excited along with the rest of Performing Arts to present this beautifully restored room as our gift to the living Christ on his milestone birthday.

Constructed in 1929, the ballroom hadn't received any renovations in fifty years. The makeover plan had been personally designed by Father. Members replaced carpets, installed new lighting and chandeliers, stripped and painted the walls and ceiling. The room colors were now a sea of alabaster, cream, and beige. The domed moldings, which served as wall decorations (part of the original 1929 design), had been painted dark ivory and trimmed in gold. The ballroom's new centerpiece was the sculptured front panel: two large alabaster phoenixes placed in mirror image affixed the off-white-colored wall. Their graceful plumage, stretching upward and curving inward, provided a circular frame for the Tongil mark (the twelve gates symbol of the Unification Church) placed in the middle. Teardrop-shaped crystal chandeliers beamed and glistened tiny rainbows overhead as we sang Holy Songs, eagerly waiting for True Parents[51] to arrive.

"They're coming!" a church leader announced. Rising to stand, we clapped and cheered as Father and Mother[52] made their way through the narrow "secret" passageway connecting the exterior mezzanine to the interior of the ballroom.

The New Hope Singers, the international choir created by Father that had accompanied him on his extensive speaking tours of the 1970s, sang an exuberant paean chosen especially for the day. As I accompanied the choir on the ebony Baldwin grand piano, rich, silvery waves of four-part harmony floated up and out past the chandeliers. I was secretly hoping, as always, that Father could feel our love for him in every note.

Then he walked onto the stage looking very handsome

in a grey-blue suit, white dress shirt, and garnet-colored tie. His face was beaming, reflecting the joy we felt to be in his presence. It always felt so natural to be with him.

Father began by apologizing for limiting the number of participants. Because we were still in the midst of a great battle against communism, he explained, it was not yet appropriate to have a spectacular celebration. Father went on to thank the people who could not come from the United States and around the world for their love and prayers.

He joked with us that because he was getting older, we Unification Church members would no longer pay attention to him. I remember well the delightful cooing sound of his voice as he cajoled us in English, "That's true! I think so!"

And then, he addressed the transformed ballroom:

Right now the beautiful ceiling is complaining that I haven't mentioned how lovely it has become for this day. The beautiful ceiling and moldings have the same birthday I do because they are born today and they want some attention from us. I can hear them calling to me, "Why don't you say, 'Happy Birthday, ceiling'?" You know what this ballroom looked like before restoration. It has been completely revolutionized and I designed it. I know you don't realize it but this place is sanctified and consecrated by this day. This is the only place I have designed. It doesn't matter how big or how old this building is; the people of the world in years ahead will come to see it and remember what I did here. People will come in the future to celebrate this day long after Mother and I are gone, but today you are celebrating with me. Would you like to celebrate in a more exciting way than people who will come here in the future? Look at everything here and appreciate it with your eyes. Open your mouth and your eyes and shout out.[53]

And so everyone seated on the floor turned their heads to thoroughly examine the sparkling new chamber, emitting loud "ooos" and "awws" as we marvelled at the transformed ballroom.

Father then changed his normal speaking procedure by asking us, the audience, to choose his sermon topic. His face was so expressive and charming; he exuded a tremendous warmth and love that filled the entire room. People began calling out requests, "Father's personal testimony!" said one. "Mother's testimony!" called out another. "That's good" was his reply. "The significance of Father's birthday" shouted out a third. "Not significant!" he cutely retorted, evoking laughter from the audience.

Then his questioning began to take a different tack. "What does God need?" he asked us. As I pondered my answer, an assortment of different answers rang out from the audience. It was obvious, however, that we had not provided the response Father was looking for. Finally, he told us, "God needs a nation."

He spent the next several hours explaining how God was still yearning for His ideal nation on earth:

What doesn't God have? One thing He doesn't have is a nation of His own sovereignty. So what should we do? I would like the topic to be Fatherland or Motherland of God, or Ideal Nation of God... If there is an Almighty God, would He be content to put up with today's reality, or would He do something to change the world back into its original shape? If there is someone here on earth commissioned by God to take over His mission and cause, what would that man or group claim? He would proclaim that the world's present course is in error, insisting that mankind must turn around. He must tell mankind that their direction must be entirely changed. What would be the slogan of that man? If you are clever you should be able to figure it out. If the world began in hatred and lies, then a course which is 180 degrees different would be one of absolute love, love so great that you love even your own enemy. To me that is a powerful slogan which can change the course of history. Can you find anything more powerful than this? Some might think that it is an easy answer; once you know then it seems to be an easy answer, but when you don't know what it is it seems very difficult to find. All the saints of history have searched for this answer and never found it. If you have such great love that you can love even your enemy, that power will melt everything. God needs a movement that can melt the wrong world down and change it into the right one. The entire world of religion is pursuing this one slogan, though in varying degrees. Which of all the saints do you think God would love the most? The answer is simple because there is someone who proclaimed this slogan. Jesus Christ stands like a giant because this is what he said...

The day of victory is coming when God will see His people and nation here on earth. Then He will declare His heavenly constitution. Will it be inferior to a democratic constitution? Truly there shall be a real democracy for life, liberty and the pursuit of happiness under God. There will be a right to life. Life is sacred and has the right to exist. That is the basic human right...

Today we are talking about the restoration of God's fatherland. Let us pledge ourselves to march forward for this fatherland here on earth. Those who pledge to God and True Parents that they will give themselves for the restoration of the heavenly kingdom and fatherland of God here on earth, raise your hands. Amen![54]

After he concluded, one thought stood out in my mind: Father's foremost goal was to gain a nation for God. I silently resolved to do my part in helping him attain it.

What I didn't clearly understand then, however, was that when Father talked to us about establishing "God's

Nation," he was referring to the very same Kingdom that Jesus had proclaimed to the people of Israel two thousand years earlier.[55]

Kerry K. Williams

True Father on Cheju Island

It was sometime in the late 1990s. I was brought over from the states to the training center in Cheju Island to translate for Father. I was there for several days, providing simultaneous translation in the back of the room. Father was speaking to a large crowd of Westerners, Koreans, and Japanese. My most vivid memory of being there was remembering how strongly Father spoke about God needing a nation. Like it was yesterday, I remember him saying:

"If you think God needs a nation, hold up your right hand!"

"If you think God needs a nation, hold up your left hand!"

"If you think God needs a nation, hold up both hands!"

"If you think God needs a nation, hold up your right foot!"

"If you think God needs a nation, hold up your left foot!"

"If you think God needs a nation, hold up both feet!"

"If you think God needs a nation, hold up both hands and both feet!"

Everyone was laughing at that point, but lying beneath Father's smile was a profound seriousness. We all emerged from that session knowing, without a shadow of a doubt, that God and True Father wanted a nation.[56]

Tim Elder

Commentary

In *Matthew 6*, Jesus gave us the most perfect of all prayers, because the Lord himself created it. In this prayer, he sought to kindle within our hearts a burning desire for the Kingdom to come on earth as well as in heaven.

Studying Jesus' words recorded in the Gospels reveals our Savior proclaiming the coming Kingdom in passage after passage. The Book of Matthew alone contains over forty such pronouncements. While Jesus came to establish the Kingdom in heaven, he first determined to create it here in the physical realm.

Undoubtedly, many will not easily accept this assertion, even when shown scriptural verification. Traditionalists will protest: How can we contradict two thousand years of mainstream Christian belief in the gospel as the crucifixion, death, and resurrection of Jesus Christ?

I would respond with another question: When Jesus returns, is it not possible that he might have new light to shed on his gospel? Did he not prophesy in *John 16:12* that he had more to tell us?

During their lifetimes, both Jesus and Reverend Moon were rejected and branded as heretics for preaching the message of God's coming Kingdom. The majority of Jewish leaders in first century AD, and Christian leaders in twentieth century AD, were not open to receiving the Messiah's proclamations.

Jesus spoke with great dignity as a King; he testified

to the sovereign nature of the Lord his God and radiated confidence that His Kingdom would surely be established. He travelled from town to town with his disciples, tirelessly proclaiming the good news of God's impending reign.

We see this same assurance exhibited by Reverend Moon at every stage of his ministry. He preached countless sermons brimming with boldness and certainty regarding the coming of God's Kingdom. He taught that Israel's responsibility was to accept Jesus and raise him up as their long-awaited Messiah and King. Reverend Moon explained to his disciples how God had spent four thousand years preparing a people and land for the Kingdom's commencement. If the Jewish people had recognized and attended Jesus as the Messiah, Jesus would not only have been successful in Israel, but also would have gone on to unite all the Arab nations and Asia, linking the East and West. By unifying the world under the sovereignty of God, he would have established the Kingdom of God on earth at that time.[57]

The Jewish people, however, however, did not fulfill their responsibility. Jesus was not accepted as the Messiah, and was crucified on the cross. Thus, God's Kingdom on earth was not established. However, Jesus opened the way to spiritual salvation and started Christianity, which is spiritually in the position of the Second Israel.[58]

As Christians, we believe that Jesus is the King of Kings. This majestic term indicates a ruler who has great authority over all his realm. Wouldn't his ability to govern been affirmed and expanded more rapidly had it begun with his own people?

With eternal gratitude, we acknowledge the spiritual salvation granted us sinners by Jesus' crucifixion, death, and resurrection. Jesus, being sinless, died in our place and became the saving grace of the world: "He forgave us all our sins, having canceled the charge of our legal indebtedness, which stood against us and condemned us; he has taken it away, nailing it to the cross." *(Colossians 2:14)*

But to fully accept Christ's teachings, we must also acknowledge that his long desired Kingdom on earth has not yet been established.

The returning Jesus declared in 1983 that his heir and successor would be the one to institute the constitution of the coming Kingdom:

> Once that successor is determined, the law or constitution of the Heavenly Kingdom shall be laid down to guide all activities. The law will guide heavenly citizens here on earth and into the Kingdom of Heaven in heaven.[59]

In October 2015, Reverend Moon's chosen heir, Reverend Hyung Jin Sean Moon, released "The Constitution of the United States of Cheon Il Guk." This document, largely based on the United States Constitution, contains the governmental structure of God's nation. The Kingdom will not be a socialist country or monarchy where everything belongs to the government or the king. God's Kingdom on earth will be established, "where the artificial structures of power, representing Satan, shall never again rule over mankind and humanity."[60] It will be an actual, sovereign country which will be founded on eternal truths found in Scripture. The three guiding principles of the Constitution are based on instructions given by Reverend Moon in 2001: "Article I of the Constitution of the Kingdom of Heaven is that you will not stain the blood lineage...The second point is not to violate human rights, and the third point is not to steal public money using public property for yourself."[61]

Due to the complete victory of True Father, Reverend Sun Myung Moon, the conditions were met to establish God's Kingdom on earth. Before his passing in 2012, the returning Jesus formally entrusted his kingship to his youngest son, Hyung Jin Moon. Reverend Moon also designated his grandson Shin-Joon as the third king. The position of king will be bequeathed within the physical lineage of the Lord of the Second Advent to each successive generation. It will be the solemn responsibility of the King, as the head of state of the United States of Cheon Il Guk, to preserve and protect the freedoms of the children of God.

The establishment of the Kingdom of God will mark the conclusion of Satan's kingships of past tyrannies. Because of Christ's victory in establishing God's lineage on the earth through the Three Kingships, the physical Kingdom will surely come. It is only a matter of time.

Scripture

Abraham will surely become a great and powerful nation, and all nations on earth will be blessed through him. *Genesis 18:18*

I will make your descendants as numerous as the stars in the sky and will give them all these lands, and through your offspring all nations on earth will be blessed... *Genesis 26:4*

Yes, all kings shall fall down before Him; All nations shall serve Him... May His name endure forever; may it continue as long as the sun. Then all nations will be blessed through Him, and they will call Him blessed. *Psalm 72:11,17*

Rise up, O God, judge the earth, for all the nations are Your inheritance. *Psalm 82:8*

All nations whom You have made
Shall come and worship before You, O Lord,
And shall glorify Your name. *Psalm 86:9*

The nations will fear the name of the Lord, all the kings of the earth will revere your glory. *Psalm 102:15*

In the last days the mountain of the Lord's temple will be established as chief among the mountains; it will be raised above the hills, and all nations will stream to it. *Isaiah 2:2*

When your days are fulfilled and you rest with your fathers, I will set up your seed after you, who will come from your body, and I will establish his kingdom. He shall build a house for My name, and I will establish the throne of his kingdom forever. I will be his Father, and he shall be My son. If he commits iniquity, I will chasten him with the rod of men and with the blows of the sons of men. But My mercy shall not depart from him, as I took it from Saul, whom I removed from before you. And your house and your kingdom shall be established forever before you. Your throne shall be established forever. *2 Samuel 7:12-16*

Yours, O Lord, is the greatness and the power and the glory and the victory and the majesty, indeed everything that is in the heavens and the earth; Yours is the dominion, O Lord, and You exalt Yourself as head over all. *1 Chronicles 29:11*

For God is the King of all the earth; Sing praises with a skillful psalm. God reigns over the nations, God sits on His holy throne. *Psalm 47:7-8*

The Lord has established His throne in the heavens, and His sovereignty rules over all. *Psalm 103:19*

Behold, the days are coming, says the Lord, when I will make a new covenant with the house of Israel and with the house of Judah—not according to the covenant that I made with their fathers in the day that I took them by the hand to lead them out of the land of Egypt, My covenant which they broke, though I was a husband to them, says the Lord. But this is the covenant that I will make with the house of Israel after those days, says the Lord: I will put My law in their minds, and write it on their hearts; and I will be their God, and they shall be My people. No more shall every man teach his neighbor, and every man his brother, saying, "Know the Lord," for they all shall know Me, from the least of them to the greatest of them, says the Lord. For I will forgive their iniquity, and their sin I will remember no more. *Jeremiah 31:31-34*

And in the days of these kings the God of heaven will set up a kingdom which shall never be destroyed; and the kingdom shall not be left to other people; it shall break in pieces and consume all these kingdoms, and it shall stand forever. *Daniel 2:44*

I saw in the night visions, and behold, with the clouds of heaven there came one like a son of man, and he came to the Ancient of Days and was presented before him. And to him was given dominion and glory and a kingdom, that all peoples, nations, and languages should serve him; his dominion is an everlasting dominion, which shall not pass away, and his kingdom is one that shall not be destroyed. *Daniel 7:13-14*

And the Lord will be king over all the earth; in that day the Lord will be the only one, and His name the only one. *Zechariah 14:9*

From that time Jesus began to preach, and to say, "Repent: for the kingdom of heaven is at hand." *Matthew 4:17*

Jesus went about all Galilee, teaching in their synagogues, and preaching the gospel of the kingdom, and healing all manner of sickness and all manner of disease among the people. *Matthew 4:23*

Blessed are the poor in spirit, for theirs is the kingdom of heaven. *Matthew 5:3*

But seek first the kingdom of God and His righteousness, and all these things will be added to you. *Matthew 6:33*

Jesus went through all the towns and villages, teaching in their synagogues, proclaiming the good news of the kingdom and healing every disease and sickness. *Matthew 9:35*

As you go, proclaim this message, "The kingdom of heaven has come near." *Matthew 10:7*

And this gospel of the kingdom shall be preached in all the world for a witness unto all nations; and then shall the end come. *Matthew 24:14*

Then shall the King say unto them on his right hand, "Come, ye blessed of my Father, inherit the kingdom prepared for you from the foundation of the world..." *Matthew 25:34*

Now after John was put in prison, Jesus came to Galilee, preaching the gospel of the kingdom of God, and saying, "The time is fulfilled, and the kingdom of God is at hand. Repent, and believe in the gospel." *Mark 1:14-15*

But he said, "I must proclaim the good news of the kingdom of God to the other towns also, because that is why I was sent." *Luke 4:43*

Then the seventh angel blew his trumpet, and there were loud voices in heaven, saying, "The kingdom of the world has become the kingdom of our Lord and of His Christ, and He shall reign forever and ever." *Revelation 11:15*

Then I saw a new heaven and a new earth, for the first heaven and the first earth had passed away, and there was no longer any sea. I saw the Holy City, the new Jerusalem, coming down out of heaven from God, prepared as a bride beautifully dressed for her husband. And I heard a loud voice from the throne saying, "Look! God's dwelling place is now among the people, and He will dwell with them. They will be His people, and God Himself will be with them and be their God. He will wipe every tear from their eyes. There will be no more death or mourning or crying or pain, for the old order of things has passed away." *Revelation 21:1-4*

....

Did you find your original homeland? You did not. Actually, you never had it. Your original homeland is the Kingdom of God on earth. Is there any nation on earth that can qualify as the nation of the original homeland? No, there is no such nation. Then, where can we expect to establish the original home nation? It should encompass the whole planet Earth. It shall be the Kingdom of God on earth and the Kingdom of God in heaven as well. Three major elements are required to establish a country: sovereignty, land, and people. Does God have sovereignty anywhere in the world today? No! Does God have a land to govern? No! Are there any people in the world that allows itself to be governed by God? No! Therefore, we do not have our homeland. Eventually, God should have sovereignty over a nation called Earth and a people called Humanity. Until that day, this world is actually not a fit place for human beings to live. *Sun Myung Moon 10/6/1964*

Once the sovereignty of Satan is expelled from the earth, then God, the eternal and absolute Being transcendent of time and space, will establish His sovereignty and His truth. In that day, God's truth will be absolute, and hence the purpose which it serves and the standard of goodness which it sets will both be absolute. This cosmic, all-encompassing truth will be firmly established by Christ at his Second Advent. *Exposition of the Divine Principle, Fall 4.3*

If Jesus was not crucified, he would have been a king, a king of kings, it is said. Literally he would have assumed that position, then that nation of Israel would have become a powerful central God-centered sovereignty. Then the unification of the world nation would have been accomplished. *Sun Myung Moon 2/10/1981*

When Jesus went to Jerusalem he looked at a fig tree on the road and, seeing that it bore no fruit, cursed it. Immediately, it withered away. That is the kind of consequence you would face if you are without fruit. What have you prepared for God in building the future nation? It is the fruits of your work, the central core and realization of this nation. The citizens of God's nation are not the fruits of an apple or peach. To this day, God has been unable to have

citizens in His Kingdom. Thus, He is now seeking His original citizens, the perfected citizens He could never have.
Sun Myung Moon 3/1/1991

You all have to become those who live for God's Kingdom and righteousness. However difficult your circumstances, you must be people who can fight and overcome them, remembering that God has hope in you. Only then can you be called His true sons and daughters. Then what kind of people can build God's Kingdom? They are those who can deny themselves out of a heart of concern for Him. Those who deny themselves for the sake of their society, people, nation and world are the very ones who can build His Kingdom. Further, those who live for His sake even to the point of denying their nation and the world are the ones who can build His Kingdom. Also, however sorrowful their circumstances may be, those who feel sorrow for their society, nation, world and even God rather than for themselves can build His Kingdom. Today you should not strive to satisfy your own desires, but rather must lead lives of faith and sacrifice in serving a higher purpose. Then you should attain the standard of the heart of Jesus who went through hardships for God's will and for humankind. You should advance to the position of God's true children who can comfort the broken heart of God who has gone through hardships to this day.
Cheon Seong Gyeong, p. 2310

God's most important objective is His nation. God always had a country in mind, selecting the people for that goal and educating them through the prophets. After the Fall, Satan had sovereignty over many nations but God never had His own country.

Even though God had chosen a family and a tribe, His chosen people didn't realize that He could never take a nation. Instead the ideal nation had to be created by the chosen people. God chose the people and the land but could never bless it as His own...

Whatever we may have acquired so far, God would give it up as the price to gain His nation. If God can win His country, then He is ready to exchange or sacrifice anything for it. That's His feeling. Once we have that nation and can raise our families there, we will prosper forever...

Many nationalities are represented here: from America, as well as from all over Europe and the Orient. But what is our purpose in uniting like this? Every individual here desires to make their country God's country or to find God's country, and to follow True Parents. We discovered that God is our Parent. To do the Will of our Father and live with Him is our purpose in being here. We must establish the country where we can live with God, our Parent.

...When my own parents and family went against me, I only had God's country in my mind. I was working and thinking like crazy. Everyone else called me crazy because I didn't think about anything else. Because I was thinking like God, God helped. No one else understood how anxious God has been and still is. You never realized how difficult my situation is. Do we have God's country yet? No. During the next 10 years, we have to resolve everything on the earth to a principled viewpoint. After this next decade, we will welcome the new century. What kind of concept do you have? God wants a unified world, His one nation. Who will fulfill this promise for Him? *Sun Myung Moon 11/23/1989*

CHAPTER 12

Christ protects God's Kingdom with the Rod of Iron

The Commander of the Lord's army

And it came to pass, when Joshua was by Jericho, that he lifted his eyes and looked, and behold, a Man stood opposite him with His sword drawn in His hand. And Joshua went to Him and said to Him, "Are You for us or for our adversaries?"

So He said, "No, but as Commander of the army of the Lord I have now come."

And Joshua fell on his face to the earth and worshiped, and said to Him, "What does my Lord say to His servant?"

Then the Commander of the Lord's army said to Joshua, "Take your sandal off your foot, for the place where you stand is holy." And Joshua did so. *Joshua 5:13-15*

Sell Your Cloak and Buy a Sword

Then Jesus asked them, "When I sent you without purse, bag or sandals, did you lack anything?"

"Nothing," they answered. He said to them, "But now if you have a purse, take it, and also a bag; and if you don't have a sword, sell your cloak and buy one. It is written:

And he was numbered with the transgressors; and I tell you that this must be fulfilled in me. Yes, what is written about me is reaching its fulfillment."

The disciples said, "See, Lord, here are two swords."

"That's enough!" he replied. *Luke 22:35-38*

Yoido Island: World Rally for Korean Freedom

With the fall of South Vietnam to the North Vietnamese on April 30, 1975, Kim Il Sung began to believe that the U.S. had shown its weakness and that reunification of Korea under his regime was finally possible. Based on his atheistic "Juche" ideology, Kim Il Sung had created a severely Stalinist regime in North Korea, and was eager to claim the entire peninsula.

In response to this threat, Reverend Moon was determined to stage a massive rally in Seoul, less than two months after South Vietnam's defeat. He was resolute to safeguard not only his fellow Koreans; he was also resolute to defend God his Father.

Korean, Japanese, American and European Unificationists distributed nearly 5 million leaflets, and over 1,000 chartered buses were used for transport from local cities and provinces. The rally itself was a staggering spectacle. A million Korean flags were distributed, and 2,400 police were mobilized for crowd control.

More than one million people had arrived at the Plaza before the June 7 rally began. The day was overcast as winding lines of buses steadily streamed into the fairgrounds. The stage, built enormously high above the ground, was filled with performers, Reverend Moon's family, and church leaders from 63 nations. After opening entertainment had concluded, the entire crowd solemnly stood as the band played the Korean national anthem.

A young Vietnamese woman walked onto the stage and gave her testimony of tremendous suffering, bursting into tears and sobbing as she shared how her parents had been killed by communists during the war. Moved by her sorrowful appeal, some patriotic young Korean men pledged their lives to defend their country by writing a solemn oath in their own blood.

Finally, Reverend Moon was introduced, and the crowd responded with thunderous applause. He strode purposefully to the podium, deeply serious, yet bearing a serene smile. The crowd listened with rapt attention as he spoke with the fiery voice of a prophet:

June 7, 1975 is the day of a new historical declaration both for me and for God...There have already been many rallies for the total unity of national security. However, this World Rally for Korean Freedom is a most unique historical convention in two senses. First, today's rally is the only convention which blames Kim Il Sung not only in the name of the people and of mankind, but also in the name of God.

Secondly, this rally is a worldwide convention where not only our Korean people gather, but also some one thousand representatives from 60 countries of different languages and cultures gather together to resolve the protection of free Korea and the whole world...
What is Communism? We know very well that Communism began with the Bolshevik Revolution in 1917, engulfing more than half of the world within the last half-century and inflicting its ruthless and savage actions upon mankind. Communism is a dreadful, satanic philosophy, whose actions are horribly criminal and destructive...Communism is not only the enemy of mankind, but more significantly it is the enemy of God. Communism is not only an ideological system of politics and economics, but it is also a form of religion based on atheism. Communism completely controls human thinking, action and way of life, which is the unique force that only a religion can have. Communism is a religion insisting that there is no God...
Today we must increase our national power. We must equip our armed forces. We must fortify our defense line. However, what is more important is to be armed with truth, that is to say, our spirit should be armed with faith and ideology. We should be armed with the ideology that there is a God and our spirit should be armed with the faith and resolution that we will fight at the cost of our lives to fulfill God's will. We can win victo-

ry over the Communists' false faith and ideology only through true faith and ideology...

In the Old Testament, nine foot Goliath stood stately with a spear in his hand. Before him was the boy David with a stone in his hand. Today we should hear David's cry. He neither cried, "You, foe, receive my stone," nor "Though I am very small, I am very strong. Come and fight with me." David cried, "I am facing you in the name of Jehovah." David defeated the giant Goliath with God's power. We should defeat Kim Il Sung, smash Mao Tse Tung, and crush the Soviet Union in the name of God. We can gain victory only through faith. Let us fortify our defense line, completely and bravely. And let us fight to the last at the cost of our lives in the holy battle for God. The final victory will be ours at last. God is on our side...

Be strongly united in the name of God. Let us rise up! Let us march on together! Let us go forward together! Thank you very much.[62]

Religious leaders from various Christian and Buddhist denominations came to the platform to declare their support for the freedom-fighting efforts of Reverend Moon. Korean flags were thrust high in the air as audience members cheered and clapped to show their united desire to maintain a communist-free nation.

Father, Sons, and the Rod of Iron

It was 1993 when we got the first working production prototype of the Kahr K9. Kook Jin nim,[63] myself, John Chamley, [64] and the staff at Saeilo[65] had been working long hours to work the bugs out of the previous prototypes. We were designing features which would get all the different parts working in a way that was functional, easy to assemble and manufacture, as well as be reliable and accurate. After a lot of hard work, we finally had something really good.

Kook Jin nim's motivation to create the Kahr pistol started because nobody made a 9 mm pistol as small as he wanted. He knew there was a better way to do it, and he was determined to figure it out. Kook Jin nim had graduated from Harvard magna cum laude in 1992, and been appointed by Father to take over Saeilo. At the same time he was designing the K9, he put Saeilo in the black (it had been running at a deficit for years), and was also working on his MBA.

So finally we had a working prototype. Kook Jin nim took it home to East Garden and waited for the opportunity to show Father. Father looked at it, and said, "This is great! Let's go to Barrytown and shoot it!" On that particular day, however, a blizzard was working its way through the northeast United States, in what would afterwards be remembered as "the storm of the century." In upstate New York, the snow was falling too fast to keep the roads plowed. But Father still wanted to go to Barrytown. Everyone told him, "Father, we can't go. There's a huge blizzard outside!" But

Father said again, adamantly, "We're going to Barrytown."

Prior to that day, Kwon Jin nim[66] had built a crew cab, F250, diesel, with a lift kit and 35 inch tires. It was a beautiful truck. Kwon Jin nim said, "Father, I'll take you to Barrytown!" So, they all piled into his pickup truck. Father sat in the back seat next to Kook Jin nim. A security guard rode up in front with Kwon Jin nim, who was primed and ready to chauffeur his father through the white tempest.

They arrived mid-afternoon at the Seminary property, and drove back to the hay barn which had formerly been used by the Christian Brothers (the previous owners) to house dairy cows. The barn had been empty and deserted since the church acquired the property in 1975. As Director of UTS[67] Security, an important part of my job was to take care of the True Children when they came onto the property. I wanted to create a place where they felt comfortable and safe, so I had transformed the basement of the barn into a makeshift shooting range. Despite being a very humble facility, Hyo Jin nim, Hyun Jin nim, and Kook Jin nim visited on a regular basis. They had inherited their Father's appreciation of firearms, and we spent countless hours in the basement of the barn improving our shooting skills. After Kook Jin nim began working on the K9 prototype, he visited almost daily.

It was an amazing time, but was now even more amazing because Father had arrived amidst a fierce snowstorm at 10 Dock Road to shoot his son's newly created pistol.

When we entered the barn, Kook Jin nim showed Father the set up. I had constructed a backstop by building a box made out of plywood (4'x4'x8'), placing it on supports two feet from the floor, then filling it with discarded newspapers from the library. Having experimented with terminal ballistics since high school, I knew how to make it safe.

We loaded some magazines, and Father began firing the K9. He emptied several magazines, while Kook Jin nim explained the various unique features of the new gun he had created. After shooting the K9, Kook Jin nim then brought out other guns for Father to try. He fired those as well; eventually we all took turns practicing with the various guns. Father was a good shot; it was obvious he knew his way around firearms.

I remember how Father really seemed to be enjoying himself, and especially how proud he was of his sons.[68]

Doug Williams

Commentary

The Commander of the Lord's army, who appeared to Joshua before the fall of Jericho, was Jesus Christ bearing the Rod of Iron.[69] The Commander could not have been an angel, because he gave no rebuke when Joshua fell down to worship at his feet. (In *Revelation 22:8-9*, the angel reproached John the apostle for bowing to him, stating that men should only worship God.)

In *Joshua 5:13-15*, Jesus manifested himself as a warrior

ruler, "with a sword drawn in his hand." He wielded the Rod of Iron on behalf of God the Father, who was preparing Joshua for battle. Jesus was making sure Joshua understood that it was God, not Joshua, who would be leading the battle. Telling Joshua to take off his shoes because he was on holy ground provided great assurance to the leader of the Israelites. Just as God had been with Moses at the burning bush, *(Exodus 3:1-6)*, so too would He be with Moses' successor.

The Jesus who appeared as the Commander of the Lord's army was the same Jesus who was born on earth over one thousand years later. Should we be surprised, then, to learn that Christ's disciples carried swords with his full knowledge? The direction given in *Luke 22:36* was in direct defiance of Roman precepts; purchasing swords was considered a capital offense. Chuck Baldwin explains in his book *To Keep or Not to Keep: Why Christians Should Not Give Up Their Guns:*

> ...during the years Jesus led his disciples, he knew his disciples carried swords illegally. Yet, he never ordered them not to carry swords. Similarly, the disciples never gave up their swords in face of the Roman law, and when Jesus told them each to buy one, they intended to obey Jesus rather than the Roman law.[70]

Jesus' direction to procure swords is amazingly bold in light of the fact that Jews were forbidden to carry swords under penalty of death.[71] Wielding a self-made leather whip to drive out the money changers from the temple *(Matthew 21:12-17)*, as well as supporting the death penalty for child abusers *(Luke 17:2)* provide further evidence that God's love and justice have more than one expression.

When Jesus chastised Peter for slashing the ear of the High Priest's servant, it was not an overall rejection of swords. Jesus scolded Peter because his chief apostle was acting against God's plan for salvation. Cutting off the ear of the servant demonstrated resistance to God's will, which was now the crucifixion.

Christians often incorrectly interpret "live by the sword, die by the sword" *(Matthew 26:52)* to mean Biblical disapproval of using weapons for defense. The phrase "live by the sword, die by the sword" means that violence should not be a life pattern. But there comes a time to fight back and defend oneself and others from harm. God commanded Deborah to call out ten thousand Israelite soldiers to defeat the technologically superior Canaanites *(Judges 4)*. He gave Gideon the courage to battle and conquer the Baal-worshiping Midianites *(Judges 6)*. Purpose and reason are the determining factors for "right" or "wrong," not the use of the weapons themselves.[72]

Jesus mandated his disciples to sell their cloaks if necessary to purchase swords (military weapons of his day) for defense. His order to exchange cloaks for swords was an urgent command, for cloaks were also used as the blankets people slept in during the cold nights of the desert. Jesus' belief in peace through strength conveys the Father's desire to protect His children, as described by David in *2 Samuel 22:3-4*:

> My God is my rock, in whom I take refuge,
> my shield and the horn of my salvation.
> He is my stronghold, my refuge and my savior--
> from violent people you save me.
> I called to the Lord, who is worthy of praise,
> and have been saved from my enemies.

Reverend Moon is remembered as a revolutionary man of peace. His tireless efforts to unite people of different faiths, nationalities and races under God was the fulfillment of Christ's longing heart as described in *Matthew 23:37*. Like Jesus of Nazareth, he also advocated providing God's people with the means to defend themselves.

When freed by the American forces from Hungnam prison in 1950, Reverend Moon journeyed to South Korea, and established the Holy Spirit Association for the Unification of World Christianity in 1954. He also created one of the first gun companies, making air rifles and eventually going on to create businesses that produced the Vulcan Cannon, M-1 rifles, and other military parts for the Defense Department of South Korea.

Reverend Moon boldly proclaimed at the Yoido Island

Rally that God's people needed both physical and spiritual protection against the forces of evil. He encouraged Koreans to be armed with faith and ideology, and also equipped with weapons of self-defense. Through his speech we can understand that the "Rod of Iron" referred to in *Revelation 2:27* has two distinct meanings: the Word of God, as well as the physical means by which to protect and defend the people who uphold it.

Six years before the rally he spoke passionately about the need for his followers to take an interest in munitions:

All Unificationists must take an interest in guns now that I am doing business with guns while on earth. Why am I involved with guns? The satanic world has done its conquering with guns. Conquering the world with guns is not our intent, but we must bear arms and create a strong protective fence. Future generations will wonder why I was interested in guns. We absolutely need them to create a defensive fence to shield ourselves from satanic world attacks. That is why I am interested in guns.[73]

In 1976 he reaffirmed this perspective:

Is it a crime to defend yourself and the heavenly nation? You should not have some naive concept of Christian love. That does not apply in a confrontation with Satan's forces, which are determined to destroy

God's world and God's people. If God has no power to defeat a satanic attack then He is no longer God. As God's force, we shall be able to defend ourselves and to defend the godly world.[74]

It was common knowledge among Unificationists that Reverend Moon loved to fish, but many were not aware of the fact that he also greatly enjoyed hunting. He often went boar and pheasant hunting on Cheju Island when in Korea. His great enthusiasm for his son Kook Jin's development of the K9 was borne out of a long-held respect and appreciation of firearms.

Although not widely publicized, Reverend Moon also spoke in his later years of the importance of firearms for maintaining peace, both before and after the Kingdom was established:

> Considering how I opened the way for weapons development here in South Korea, how much propaganda has been put out about me, centering on the idea that I am some sort of murderer. At this time, we are now at the point where we go over the top of this. On the contrary, those weapons can become the source and origin of peace. My son Kook-Jin-i developed a type of pistol...[75]

In the future, when we have a nation in Cheon Il Guk, will we need to have guns, or not need to have guns?

(Congregation: We'll need them.) Do police officers need to have guns, or not need to have guns? (They need them.)...Think about it. If you do not have the capacity to protect yourself at any time, then you get attacked and invaded. If you haven't trained to protect yourself, you can run into an accident and end up dead. Do you see? (Yes.)

If you go down to South America and a tiger comes up and bites into you, you'll die. So, do you think we have to train with guns, or not train with guns? (We have to train with guns.) If you go into the mountains and come across a lot of wild boars, they will run at you and attack you, and you end up dead. So, even if you don't want to do it, you have to train with guns. If you want to go anywhere in the world, that is.

The gun developed by my Kook Jin-i, that's the best kind of gun for protecting yourself. Women can just pop them in their purses. That kind of gun is a gun of peace. When men come along, when thieves come along, the woman tells them to wait for a moment--I've wrapped my valuables, my money up in this white cloth here–but she's actually got her gun wrapped up in it. She says, "I'll get my valuables for you. I just need to get them out of this white cloth here, so just wait a moment, then... surprise! You dirty bastard!" Day or night, he has nowhere to run to. Women are training themselves in this manner, even if no one here knows about it, though...[76]

The Kingdom of Heaven is the rule of the Rod of Iron within the Christian framework. Both Jesus and Reverend Moon demonstrated the belief that a real kingdom needs real protection. They both personally experienced the brutal consequences of being unarmed when faced by tyrants. More than anyone else, Christ knows that for God's Kingdom to come, godly people must be able to wield stronger "fire-power" than the forces of evil *(Revelation 20:9)*. The last book of the New Testament depicts the Rod of Iron as a salient accoutrement of kingdom governance. As the establishment of the physical Kingdom draws near, God's people must stay vigilant and be prepared to defend themselves against all those who would try to usurp their freedom.

Scripture

So He drove out the man; and He placed cherubim at the east of the garden of Eden, and a flaming sword which turned every way, to guard the way to the tree of life. *Genesis 3:24*

Therefore I stationed some of the people behind the lowest points of the wall at the exposed places, posting them by families, with their swords, spears and bows. After I looked things over, I stood up and said to the nobles, the officials and the rest of the people, "Don't be afraid of them. Remember the Lord, who is great and awesome, and fight for your families, your sons and your daughters, your wives and your homes."

When our enemies heard that we were aware of their plot and that God had frustrated it, we all returned to the wall, each to our own work.

From that day on, half of my men did the work, while the other half were equipped with spears, shields, bows and armor. The officers posted themselves behind all the people of Judah who were building the wall. Those who carried materials did their work with one hand and held a weapon in the other, and each of the builders wore his sword at his side as he worked. But the man who sounded the trumpet stayed with me.

Then I said to the nobles, the officials and the rest of the people, "The work is extensive and spread out, and we are widely separated from each other along the wall. Wherever you hear the sound of the trumpet, join us there. Our God will fight for us!"

So we continued the work with half the men holding spears, from the first light of dawn till the stars came out. At that time I also said to the people, "Have every man and his helper stay inside Jerusalem at night, so they can serve us as guards by night and as workers by day." Neither I nor my brothers nor my men nor the guards with me took off our clothes; each had his weapon, even when he went for water. *Nehemiah 4:13-23*

Ask of Me, and I will give you
The nations for Your inheritance,
And the ends of the earth for your possession.
You shall break them with a rod of iron;
You shall dash them to pieces like a potter's vessel.
Psalm 2:8-9

Even though I walk through the valley of the shadow of death, I will fear no evil, for you are with me; your rod and your staff, they comfort me. *Psalm 23:4*

And he shall rule them with a rod of iron; as the vessels of a potter shall they be broken to shivers: even as I received of my Father. *Revelation 2:27*

And she brought forth a man child, who was to rule all nations with a rod of iron: and her child was caught up unto God, and to his throne. *Revelation 12:5*

Now out of his mouth goes a sharp sword, that with it he should strike the nations. And he himself will rule them with a rod of iron. He himself treads the winepress of the fierceness and wrath of Almighty God. *Revelation 19:15*

Let everyone be subject to the governing authorities, for there is no authority except that which God has established. The authorities that exist have been established by

God. Consequently, whoever rebels against the authority is rebelling against what God has instituted, and those who do so will bring judgment on themselves. For rulers hold no terror for those who do right, but for those who do wrong. Do you want to be free from fear of the one in authority? Then do what is right and you will be commended. For the one in authority is God's servant for your good. But if you do wrong, be afraid, for rulers do not bear the sword for no reason. They are God's servants, agents of wrath to bring punishment on the wrongdoer. *Romans 13:1-4*

Although I have worked to develop the [gun] factory over the course of twelve years, our business has dedicated itself more than any other business in Korea. God knows this. With firm resolve, I have been able to make wicked Satan retreat. This is absolutely so. I am not doing business with a self-centered motivation. God is governing the fortunes of the Korean Republic. In that the growth of the Korean economy is under God's administration, more than anyone else in Korea I am putting aside self-interest and pursuing that goal in a public way...

Looking at Korea's actual situation, surrounded by enemies on three sides, protecting the nation by establishing a proper ideological perspective is imperative. Judging from the nation's situation, the time will surely come when the Republic of Korea will regard the defense industry as important. For the past ten years, I have been preparing for that. The time has come. Since the government announced it will strengthen the nation's military, people are busy building factories here and there. We are producing air guns that look the same as the M1 rifle and sending some to the Blue House. We must begin producing rifles to be used for training in middle and high schools and also rifles of a new type. That is why I have instructed that this year's production goal be accomplished no matter how difficult it is to achieve.

This year we sent two thousand five hundred guns to Japan. I instructed our agents to spread throughout Japan and do as I say. I told them, "Without a doubt this can be accomplished. Be confident. Selling them won't be difficult. If you are confident you can succeed."

This year we also sent five hundred guns to the United States. Yet, our missionaries there, Bong Choon Choi [Sang Ik "Papasan" Choi] and Young Oon Kim, objected and asked me to please not send the guns.

I said, "What do you mean, please don't send them? If you don't do it, I will do it even if it means going there myself. Please just do as I ask." If I tell them that we sent fifteen thousand guns to Japan, members in the United States would say, "Oh my!" If I told them that we had sold fifty thousand or one hundred thousand guns in Japan, the American members would feel compelled to sell even more than that. I went around the United States and investigated. America is a golden market; it is virgin soil.

There are unlimited resources there, which is why it is possible to sell more than these numbers.

In the future, we must go out to the world. By the end of this year, or at the latest, next April, we will have missions in forty nations. You may not be aware of this, but missionaries have already gone out to Norway, Sweden, Denmark, Greece and other locations. If I tell them where I had designated holy grounds during my world tour, they will go there. We have missions in many nations in Africa. In the future, within three or four years at the latest, we will have missions in 360 foreign locations. I will send missionaries to those unknown nations, nations that are not registered with the United Nations. How will I send them? They cannot take money. They can take our air rifles with them. *Sun Myung Moon 7/9/1969*

Then can people in your nation have an easy mind when the enemies have formidable weapons? No! It is better for you to manufacture heavy armaments, strengthen your army, and wait without declaring war. They will find you stronger than they are; they cannot attack you. We must advocate the manufacturing of armaments. Then, what if the existing churches will protest against us saying that we are advocating the manufacturing of armaments and weapons? Communism, being the ultimate and greatest enemy to God, must be shattered into pieces first. After that, all the rest of the satans must be annihilated from the face of the earth. Any other opposing groups will be either digested or swallowed up by us or annihilated. *Sun Myung Moon 3/16/1975*

If the communists come to destroy the Unification Church with guns then we will have to fight with guns too. We can't be their helpless victims and be defeated by their bullets. Do you think God will win such a battle for you? If the time comes to fight the satanic force, I will never hesitate to become the commander-in-chief and lead the heavenly army into battle. Do you think the Defense Department can safeguard God's world? Don't trust it too much. You can only trust the heavenly forces that are dedicated to God's purpose. Our young people should be trained in every way physically. In a final war against the satanic force it will be a life or death battle. In order to safeguard the heavenly side we may need to become soldiers. It is Satan's nature that once he feels he is in a superior position he will attack. Is it a crime to defend yourself and the heavenly nation? You should not have some naive concept of Christian love. That does not apply in a confrontation with Satan's forces, which are determined to destroy God's world and God's people. If God has no power to defeat a satanic attack then He is no longer God. As God's force, we shall be able to defend ourselves and to defend the godly world. We are a different kind of religious leadership. *Sun Myung Moon 11/21/1976*

CHAPTER 13

Through Christ, we receive God's grace to become co-heirs of His Kingdom

The gift of incredible grace

As mentioned in chapter 11, the returning Jesus announced in 1983 that his chosen heir would be the one to release the actual Constitution of the Kingdom of Heaven. In that same speech, he also stated that "a physical representative of the True Father" would always remain on earth. From one generation to another, this central co-heir, who also shares Christ's bloodline, would be the "axis on which the earth will turn."[77]

Thirty-two years later, the day for releasing the Kingdom Constitution had finally arrived. On October 11, 2015, at Sanctuary Church in Newfoundland Pennsylvania, Reverend Hyung Jin Sean Moon, the thrice-anointed successor of the returning Christ,[78] stood on a dais in the church lobby. The normally humble setting had been transformed into a palatial environment. Dressed in a regal white robe, bearing a golden crown, the Second King read through "The Constitution of the United States of Cheon Il Guk" in a calm, decisive voice. At the conclusion, he invited his Queen, Yeonah, who had been listening attentively throughout, to join him. They stood facing one another, eyes closed, hand in hand, as he prayed:

> Our dearest most beloved Heavenly Father,
> Father, the Kingdom of God, the free and ideal world, which You intended to bestow upon Your children in the Garden of Eden, Father, is the final Kingdom, the Kingdom where Your children will be able to truly be free, to live by conscience, live with responsibility, to serve one another, and to serve and love their God. All the rights and enumerations today declared in "The Constitution of the United States of Cheon Il Guk" are the gift of Your incredible grace.
>
> Father, a land which will be the most free and prosperous land, a land where no one organ of the government may monopolize power, a land where Your blood lineage is alive, a land where your covenant between You and Your people are protected by the kingships.
>
> Father, we thank You because as Christ, You took on the path of the ten thousand crosses, to prepare the way for a sovereign state, a sovereign nation, where the people of God could live in accordance with the divine edicts and eternal truths which come from their Creator.
>
> Father, a place where it is impossible for the hierarchy and or the bureaucracies to take control of the master position and to leave their proper positions as servants, a place where monopolies and concentrations

of power which Satan has used throughout the entire course of time to dominate and manipulate markets, to dominate and manipulate polities and nation states, a place where we will be free as a people from such intrusions.

Father, we thank You this day of the Constitution that has been released into the atmosphere for the future generations, and the one day future actual sovereign nation which will institute this politically and legally, and bring into the actual fruit and fruition of Providence, a Kingdom of Heaven, a Kingdom of God on Earth.

Father, we pray for that future day because we know that in this time of tribulation, that we are being led by Your spirit and by Your immeasurable and amazing grace. Father we thank You this day for all the patriots that are gathered here and now the founding fathers of the nation that are standing here. We eagerly await the actual institution of that day where we can actually be citizens of a nation, a nation which is more free, and a nation where the citizens exercise their creativity, responsibility, and responsibilities to serve one another and to create the most prosperous, the most abundant, and the most fruitful nation in all world history.

Father, it is with those kind of blessings that so many intrusions and invasions of different philosophies that try to manipulate and use power and gradually use public opinion to steal away slowly by promising free things to people and accruing power, eventually taking the position of owner and becoming the master of the nation.

Father, it is in this Constitution that is given to us as the covenant of You and Your peoples, that that block and that restriction upon the government of doing such things will be instituted, and it will be a place where all the concentrations of power will find more and more impediments of rooting themselves and taking over the proper position into which they are to be kept.

Father, we thank You for the Divine Principle and the Eight Textbook curriculum which is the foundation of this Constitution. We thank You for the eternal Biblical scripture which is the eternal foundation of Your foundation as the Lord of the Second Advent.

Heavenly Father, thank You for your incredible love and mercy upon us as we look with high anticipation, even though we may be mocked, we may be scorned and we may be attacked. Our faith and our love in You and our yearning for the Kingdom of God on Earth shall never wane.

We thank You once again, and we give You all the praise, glory and honor, we report this in our names as central blessed families, and I report this in the name of Moon Hyung Jin, with the authority of the Three Kingships, in Your precious name we pray, Amen and Aju.[79]

After receiving flowers, and giving three cheers of "Og Mansei," the Second King and Queen exited to the victorious strains of Handel's "Hallelujah Chorus." With the releasing of "The Constitution of the United States of Cheon Il Guk" through his anointed heir, Christ was finally able to bequeath the structure of the heavenly government by which we could join him as co-heirs.

The Second King explains Romans 8:17

Sanctuary Church had been selected as one of the subjects of the A & E[80] documentary "Cults and Extreme Beliefs," scheduled for release in Summer 2018. The Newfoundland Church main sanctuary stage, normally the setting for Sunday sermons and worship music, had been temporarily transformed into a TV studio. A & E interviewer Elizabeth Vargas and the Second King, sitting face-to-face only a few feet apart, were surrounded by lights and cameras ready to record the proceedings. Vargas was straightforward in her questioning:

"Your father claimed to be humanity's savior. Do you also claim to be humanity's savior?"

"No. I'm just his heir and successor."

"So he's still the savior?"

"Yes, he holds that unique position."

"So are you a spokesperson, a prophet?"

"He designated a kingship. He chose one of my children; he designated a kingly line. He chose my son to be his heir and representative in the third generation."

The Second King went on to describe his position as somewhat akin to the role of the Pope in the Catholic Church, clarifying that he did not agree with the Vatican's structure of centralized governance. When challenged by Vargas that bearing the title of "Third King" was a heavy burden for his thirteen-year-old son, the Second King replied:

> We see it from a Biblical context. In Romans 8:17, Christ talks about being co-heirs with Christ; he says you are inheritors with God, and that you will rule with Christ. When we talk about the Kingdom of God, that is a place where the normal citizen is also a king or queen. It's a nation of kings. It's a nation of queens. And so it's a nation that stands with the King of Kings, and with his Kingship line. The citizens have kingly rights; they have the rights that kings have enjoyed through what we call fallen or satanic history (coming from a Judeo-Christian background). In the Kingdom, it's different from our normal view of kingship lines, with centralized monarchies. We see the Kingdom of God as very decentralized, where the citizens also have the rights of kings. In a nutshell, the right of territory, the right to be free from taxation, the right to be armed, and to have a territory that is protected.[81]

Vargas then returned to her earlier line of questioning by once again probing the Second King's thoughts on the identity of his father:

"But your dad said he had a more elevated, more important position as savior of humanity."

"Right. Lord of the Second Advent, or returning Christ."

"Then that makes your father God."

"It makes him the returning Jesus."

"Then what does that make you?"

The Second King smiled slightly before he spoke, "His son. It makes me his heir and successor. It doesn't make me the Messiah or the Savior."

Vargas' voice rang with a note of incredulity as she asked, "Was your father the Messiah?"

"Yes, we see him as the Messiah, basically the returning Jesus, the returning Christ."[82]

Pastor Sean spoke simply as he made his point crystal clear: both the position of Second King and the position of fellow co-heir originated from the unmerited grace of God. And that grace had been bestowed through the returning Jesus, the Reverend Sun Myung Moon.

Commentary

Jesus, the only begotten Son of God, is the natural heir of the Father. God speaks to us through His Son whom He has "appointed heir of all things" *(Hebrews 1:2)*.

The Messiah is the person deserving the "estate" of the

Creator. He is the one who has lived a life of absolute love, absolute faith, and absolute obedience to God. It is natural for a father to bequeath his inheritance to his most faithful child. As descendants of the false father, we all bear the lineage of the one who abandoned God. We are liars if we claim not to have sinned against our sinless, perfect Father *(1 John 1:10)*.

When we accept and submit to Jesus as our Lord and Savior, however, God no longer treats us as sinners deserving of death *(Romans 3:23; 6:23)*, but looks upon us with love and grace *(Ephesians 2:8–9)*. God puts our sin completely out of view and replaces it with His own righteousness. Although undeserving, we are placed in the position to inherit everything that belongs to Christ. When we are born again, we become a son or daughter of the most high God, and a joint heir with Jesus. What belongs to Jesus will also belong to us; we are welcomed into God's family as one of His children. "So you are no longer a slave, but God's child; and since you are his child, God has made you also an heir." *(Galatians 4:7)*

To understand our role as co-heirs, we must know what kind of kingdom we will be inheriting. Some Christians purport that the Kingdom already exists through the person of Jesus. Others also believe it is comprised of people whose hearts and minds have been faithful to the teachings of Christ. Still others claim that the Church, the body of Christ, constitutes the Kingdom. Another group professes that the Kingdom will begin when Jesus literally comes on the clouds of heaven and our resurrected bodies rise up to meet him.

As mentioned earlier, the Lord's Prayer in *Matthew 6* indicates that the Kingdom is a real nation that will come physically as well as spiritually. Through Jesus, God was intending to fulfill the prophecy written by Daniel over five hundred years earlier:

> And in the days of these kings the God of heaven will set up a kingdom which shall never be destroyed; and the kingdom shall not be left to other people; it shall break in pieces and consume all these kingdoms, and it shall stand forever. *Daniel 2:44*

As the Second King prayed on October 11, 2015, God's nation will be a land resembling the ideal world God intended to bestow upon His children in the Garden of Eden. The adoption and implementation of "The Constitution of the United States of Cheon Il Guk" will make it possible to actualize the culture of the Kingdom. This Constitution is absolutely necessary to safeguard the citizens' ability to fulfill their God-given roles of sovereign kings and queens. By placing concrete restrictions on the growth of government, archangelic power is prevented from coalescing into a centralized force. No one organ of government will be able to monopolize power. The ten rights of Principle

II (adopted verbatim from the Bill of Rights) highlight the freedoms from governmental control which are to be afforded all citizens of Cheon Il Guk.

As explained earlier, Christ will maintain his presence and authority on earth through his *teshinja* (representative body). The teshinja is selected by the presiding King for each ensuing generation, and will be a direct descendant within the lineage of Hyung Jin Sean Moon. The teshinja serves as the monarch of Cheon Il Guk. The presiding monarch, or King, functions within the judicial branch of government as its only lifetime appointment. His responsibilities are articulated in Principle III, Article I of "The Constitution of the United States of Cheon Il Guk." An example of humankind's co-heirship with Christ can be seen in the manner of appointing Supreme Court judges. Although they are selected by the King, the consent of the Senate is required for approval.

Reverend Sun Myung Moon is the First King of Cheon Il Guk, "the King of Kings and Lord of Lords" described in *Revelation 19:16*. The Second King of Cheon Il Guk, Reverend Hyung Jin Sean Moon, made it clear in the A & E documentary that he, Hyung Jin, is not the Messiah. Rather, he was chosen by the Messiah to be the bearer of the kingly lineage, as well as the preserver of his Father's teachings and traditions. True Father could give the Constitution of Cheon Il Guk to Hyung Jin because of his son's absolute faith and filial piety towards the man he fully recognized and attended as the Lord of the Second Advent.

There will be great freedom within the Kingdom to exercise the immutable and inalienable rights given to us by our Creator. Just as Jesus never used political power to force anyone to act morally, no one in the Kingdom will be coerced to adhere to a particular set of beliefs. We can anticipate laws to be enacted that will support the principles of the Constitution. Most importantly, people will be able to live from the victory of Christ and fulfill their roles as responsible citizens of Heaven.

In the Kingdom, Christ and his co-heirs will protect their authority with the Rod of Iron *(Psalm 2:8-9, Revelation 2:27, Revelation 12:5, Revelation 19:15).* Once the sword, and now the modern-day firearm, the Rod of Iron is necessary to remain vigilant against the powers of darkness. Because man has free will, there is always the possibility for evil to manifest. Revelation 20 tells us even after the returning Christ has reigned for one thousand years, Satan will rise again to war against the forces of goodness. A vicious enemy named Gog and Magog will gather Satan's people together, "the number of whom is as the sand of the sea" *(Revelation 20:8).*

As the King of Kings, Christ is the King of people who have the rights of monarchs. One of a king's primary functions is to protect his domain, and no kingdom can be secured without arming its people. When Christ gave us the Rod of Iron, he liberated us from slavery and showed us how to live as a free people. With this vital accoutrement, the citizens will have the means by which to defend their personal territory. It will be the responsibility of armed kings and queens, the sovereign peoples of Cheon Il Guk, to maintain peace. The locus of power will no longer reside within the government; it will shift to the citizens of the Kingdom.

In 2006, Reverend Moon created the foundation for this future transfer of force by establishing the Peace Kingdom Corps and the Peace Kingdom Police. In his inaugural speech, Reverend Moon instructed all those who will bear arms in the Kingdom to protect the earth on behalf of God. He encouraged them to become righteous police and military by focusing on Christ and his Word.[83]

The second fundamental accoutrement of the Kingdom, bequeathed by the grace of God, is the crown. In *Revelation 3:11,* Jesus tells us, "Behold, I am coming quickly! Hold fast what you have, that no one may take your crown." James, Paul, Timothy, and Peter all wrote of the crown bequeathed by Christ. They explained that the crown may be worn by those who love Christ and desire his Second Coming *(2 Timothy 4:8, Thessalonians 2:19).* Those worthy of the crown will endure temptation *(James 1:2),* practice self-control as they strive for mastery in all things *(1 Corinthians 9:25-27),* and "shepherd the flock" by serving and caring for others *(1 Peter 5:2-4).*

As co-heirs, we take responsibility on behalf of Jesus

to maintain the Kingdom. Christ gives us the ends of the earth for our possession *(Psalm 2:8-9)* not so we can live selfishly, but so that we will exercise responsible stewardship on his behalf. In the physical Kingdom on earth, families will designate a kingship line within their tribe which is centrally responsible for maintaining allegiance to Christ. Tribal kings must teach each successive generation that apart from Christ's authority, their kingship means nothing.

The crown does not symbolize our greatness, but the fact that we have been crucified along with Christ, who now lives within us *(Galatians 2:20)*. Because Christ loved me and gave himself for me, I claim my authority as co-heir by giving myself fully to him.

Scripture

But the meek shall inherit the earth,
And shall delight themselves in the abundance of peace.
Psalm 37:11

And Jesus said to them, "Truly I say to you, that you who have followed me, in the regeneration when the Son of Man will sit on His glorious throne, you also shall sit upon twelve thrones, judging the twelve tribes of Israel."
Matthew 19:28

Then the King will say to those on his right, "Come, you who are blessed by my Father; take your inheritance, the kingdom prepared for you since the creation of the world." *Matthew 25:34*

Then the eleven disciples went to Galilee, to the mountain where Jesus had told them to go. When they saw him, they worshiped him; but some doubted. Then Jesus came to them and said, "All authority in heaven and on earth has been given to me. Therefore, go and make disciples of all nations, baptizing them in the name of the Father and of the Son and of the Holy Spirit, and teaching them to obey everything I have commanded you. And surely I am with you always, to the very end of the age." *Matthew 28:16-20*

Yet to all who did receive him, to those who believed in his name, he gave the right to become children of God. *John 1:12*

For the promise, that he should be the heir of the world, was not to Abraham, or to his seed, through the law, but through the righteousness of faith. *Romans 4:13*

Now if we are children, then we are heirs—heirs of God and co-heirs with Christ, if indeed we share in his sufferings in order that we may also share in his glory. *Romans 8:17*

We are therefore Christ's ambassadors, as though God were making His appeal through us. We implore you on Christ's behalf: Be reconciled to God. *2 Corinthians 5:20*

If you belong to Christ, then you are Abraham's seed, and heirs according to the promise. *Galatians 3:29*

Praise be to the God and Father of our Lord Jesus Christ! In his great mercy he has given us new birth into a living hope through the resurrection of Jesus Christ from the dead, and into an inheritance that can never perish, spoil or fade. This inheritance is kept in heaven for you... *1 Peter 1:3*

And whatever you do, do it heartily, as to the Lord and not to men, knowing that from the Lord you will receive the reward of the inheritance; for you serve the Lord Christ. *Colossians 3:23-24*

And everyone who competes for the prize is temperate in all things. Now they do it to obtain a perishable crown, but we for an imperishable crown. Therefore I run thus: not with uncertainty. Thus I fight: not as one who beats the air. But I discipline my body and bring it into subjection, lest, when I have preached to others, I myself should become disqualified. *1 Corinthians 9:25-27*

For what is our hope, or joy, or crown of rejoicing? Is it not even you in the presence of our Lord Jesus Christ at his coming? *1 Thessalonians 2:19*

Finally, there is laid up for me the crown of righteousness, which the Lord, the righteous Judge, will give to me on that Day, and not to me only but also to all who have loved his appearing. *2 Timothy 4:8*

Blessed is the man who endures temptation; for when he has been approved, he will receive the crown of life which the Lord has promised to those who love Him. *James 1:12*

Shepherd the flock of God which is among you, serving as overseers, not by compulsion but willingly, not for dishonest gain but eagerly; nor as being lords over those entrusted to you, but being examples to the flock; and when the Chief Shepherd appears, you will receive the crown of glory that does not fade away. *1 Peter 5:2-4*

I am coming soon. Hold on to what you have, so that no one will take your crown. *Revelation 3:11*

The historical ambition of God is to raise up one perfect man of God who can take care of the world. God is waiting for that one man to appear, the man the Bible promises will be the second Messiah. This one man that

God is looking for will be able to completely rise above the accusation of Satan and be victorious over all human struggle. He is the person who will inherit all of history through taking responsibility for all of mankind. We must prepare ourselves to become the coworkers of this man. *Sun Myung Moon 11/21/1976*

Inheritance is realized on the foundation of having acquired kingship. *Cheon Seong Gyeong, p. 2307*

God has worked until now to fulfill His will by saving humanity. His will is to establish His kingdom. Hence, there is no denying that He has been raising people on His side --who could become the citizens and children of that kingdom. Where is He thinking of establishing that kingdom? He is not trying to establish it in the spirit world, but on earth. Then who are the ones qualified to become the citizens of His kingdom that is to be established on earth? It is all of you. You are the center that can build the heavenly nation. *Cheon Seong Gyeong, p. 2308*

From such a perspective, what should you now seek? You must root out the elements of unrighteousness that have prevented the establishment of God's Kingdom and His righteousness, in other words, His ideal for heaven and earth. By doing so you should gain victory through the struggles in your daily life to stand in the place of His son Jesus. In other words, if you wish to become the righteous citizens of His Kingdom, you should not be foolish people who fight over what they are going to eat and wear. Rather, you should get beyond the issues of food, drink and clothing. If any of these are given to you at all, you should be able to share them with those who are naked or hungry. If you have a loaf of bread, God's heart inspires your heart to share that bread instead of eating it alone. Jesus displayed that heart but the people around him were unable to do so. *Cheon Seong Gyeong, pp. 2309-2310*

You are the nation of the ideal world of True Parents connected with the heavenly world. You are owners of this nation; you represent its sovereignty and inherit everything from God. Your families are God's heirs and representatives; you have to pass down everything from Him to all your descendants. This is not something for one age only; it's for thousands of years and numerous generations. This legacy gains greater value with the passage of time. *Sun Myung Moon 1/7/2008*

Today, at this time, there must be only one line of authority. The center, centered on Korea or on the world, over the entire Unification Church will stretch out and become larger. From now, I can leave someone in charge of my work on my behalf. Currently, there is no one among our church members who surpasses Hyung Jin in his standard of faith or in any other way. Do you understand? I am appointing him. *Sun Myung Moon 4/16/2008*

Father, people were unaware of the fact that when midnight comes after the passing of early evening, the shining hope of tomorrow that is the True Parent, the True Teacher, and the True King, the representative of the kingship of hope, and the authority of the heir to that kingship, is here. At this time of transition today, this occasion is one where they can inherit the authority as the representatives and heirs who can attend to everything on behalf of True Parents.[84] *Sun Myung Moon 4/16/2008*

I now proclaim the launch of the era of a new heaven and earth, an era after the coming of heaven, long-awaited and yearned for by billions of your ancestors in the spirit world who have come and gone in history: this is the era of the Kingdom of the Peaceful, Ideal World. Not only the four great religious founders but also billions of good ancestors have come down to earth at this point to guide you on the heavenly path. The age in which the fallen and corrupted world plays havoc on humanity, allowing those who are evil to live better than others, is passing away.

Rev. Moon, who received the seal of Heaven, has come as the True Parent of humanity and the King of Peace. I will be true to my promise to God.

I will bring to fruition the era of the Kingdom of the Peaceful, Ideal World on this earth, without fail. Therefore, please bear in mind that all of you gathered here today are the central figures in establishing the Kingdom of the

Peaceful, Ideal World on this earth, in attendance to the King and Queen of Peace, the True Parents...

Please become true princes and princesses who can attend and live together with God, the eternal peace king, as the true parent of humanity. Let us each live up to the standard of a true filial child, a patriot, a saint, and a member of the family of divine sons and daughters of God, in order to create the peace kingdom for all eternity.

Sun Myung Moon 3/16/2006

Endnotes

1 Sun Myung Moon, *As a Peace Loving Global Citizen* (Washington, D.C., The Washington Times Foundation, 2010), p. 53.

2 The *Exposition of the Divine Principle*, one of the eight canonized texts comprising the Completed Testament, is the core teaching of Reverend Moon.

3 Dinesh D'Souza, *What's So Great About Christianity* (Carol Stream, Tyndale House Publishers, Inc., 2007), p.126.

4 Sun Myung Moon, "Going Beyond 13 Summits," July 19, 2012.

5 It is the author's opinion that while on earth, the returning Christ chose to emphasize his human-like qualities, due to the fact that he was existing within a physical body. Also, by emphasizing his humanness, he gave us hope that we could overcome our sin and achieve Christ-like perfection *(Matthew 5:48)*.

6 The Eight Great Textbooks comprise the texts canonized by Reverend Sun Myung Moon. They are also referred to as The Completed Testament.

7 Sun Myung Moon, "Declaration and Will," June 5, 2010.

8 Reverend Moon designated the Three Kingships as himself, his son Hyung Jin, and his grandson Shin-Joon.

9 The Korean term Reverend Moon created which means "Kingdom of God."

10 Except for chapter 13, which contains two stories about the Second King.

11 The Completed Testament is comprised of the Eight Great Textbooks canonized by Reverend Sun Myung Moon. They are: *Cheon Seong Gyeong, Pyeong Hwa Shin Gyeong, Exposition of the Divine Principle, True Family: Gateway to Heaven, The Family Pledge, The Sermons*

of the Reverend Sun Myung Moon, World Scripture I & II, Owner of Peace and Owner of Lineage.

12 A Christophany is an appearance of God's Son before he assumed a human nature and was made man.

13 Sun Myung Moon, "Let Us Possess the Everlasting Love of the Father," October 5, 1958.

14 *Cheon Seong Gyeong*, pp.161-162.

15 *Cheon Seong Gyeong*, p.937.

16 C.S. Lewis, *Mere Christianity* (San Francisco, Harper Collins, 2001), 55-56.

17 Kyle Barton, "The History of the Liar, Lunatic, Lord Trilemma," *Conversant Faith*, May 4, 2012, https://conversantfaith.com/2012/05/04/the-history-of-liar-lunatic-lord-trilemma/

18 Sun Myung Moon, *Blessing and Ideal Family (Part 1)*, https://www.tparents.org/Moon-Books/BIF1/BIF1-1-103.htm

19 Juda Myers, "Interview with Juda Myers," The King's Report, December 14, 2017, https://www.youtube.com/watch?v=WLcTfYrgDLM

20 Michael Breen, *Sun Myung Moon: The Early Years* (West Sussex, Refuge Books, 1997), p. 37.

21 *Cheon Seong Gyeong*, described by Reverend Moon as "Heaven's Holy Scripture," is one of the Eight Great Textbooks.

22 Hyun Shil Kang, "From Evangelist to Disciple," August 1982.

23 Sun Myung Moon, "The Heart of Jesus Who Must Restore All Tasks," March 23,1958.

24 Ibid.

25 Korean word for heart, sentiment, deep love.

26 Korean word for true, sincere devotion.

27 Sun Myung Moon, "Jesus Is the Hero of the Universal Revolution," November 11, 1956.

28 The seven deaths and resurrections is a term used by the Second King to describe True Father's torturous course of six imprisonments and a helicopter crash.

29 Billy Graham, "5 Verses on Hope Found in Jesus Christ," *The Billy Graham Library*, March 23, 2016, https://billygrahamlibrary.org/5-verses-on-hope-found-in-jesus-christ/

30 Sun Myung Moon, "Part 12: Pyongyang Prison, Hungnam Labor Camp," *Sun Myung Moon's Life In His Own Words*, https://www.tparents.org/Moon-Books/SunMyungMoon-Life/SunMyung-Moon-Life-12.htm

31 Reverend Moon wrote this holy song shortly after being released from Hungnam prison. It is the national anthem of Cheon Il Guk.

32 Hyung Jin Sean Moon, "Interview with Rev. Hyung Jin Moon," January 28, 2016, https://www.youtube.com/watch?v=3X_TUviBmeI

33 Sun Myung Moon, "The Sorrowful Heart of Jesus as He Went to the Mountain," January 25, 1959.

34 Sun Myung Moon, "The Father and I," July 12, 1959.

35 Breen, Sun Myung Moon, pp. 79-80.

36 Ibid

37 Sun Myung Moon, "Part 12: Pyongyang Prison, Hungnam Labor Camp," *Sun Myung Moon's Life In His Own Words*, https://www.tparents.org/Moon-Books/SunMyungMoon-Life/SunMyung-Moon-Life-12.htm

38 Korean word for God.

39 Hyung Jin Moon, *A Bald Head and a Strawberry*, (Tarrytown, Sincerity

Publications, 2004), pp.13-15.

40 Williams, J. Douglas, Interview by author, Spring 2019.

41 Moon, Yeonah Lee, Interview by author, Spring 2018.

42 A Completed Testament Age Christian is defined by the author as a Christian who believes that Reverend Sun Myung Moon is the returning Jesus.

43 Sun Myung Moon, "The Toil of God as He Tries to Raise Up His Beloved Children," October 11, 1959.

44 Sun Myung Moon, "Change of Blood Lineage," October 13, 1970.

45 Bo Hi Pak, *Messiah: My Testimony to Rev. Sun Myung Moon Volume II*, (Lanham, University Press of America, 2002), 345-349.

46 Breen, *Sun Myung Moon*, p. 34.

47 Pak, *Messiah*, p. 338.

48 CAUSA is the Latin word for cause. CAUSA stands for the First Cause of the universe, God. In the 1980s, CAUSA was adopted as the name of Reverend Moon's world-wide ideological offensive to counter the global threat of communism.

49 The Rod of Iron has two distinct meanings: the Word of God, and the physical means by which to protect and defend the people who uphold it.

50 Abbreviation for "Holy Spirit Association for the Unification of World Christianity."

51 "True Parents" is the Unificationist term for the returning Christ and his bride *(Revelation 22:17).*

52 In 1980, Hak Ja Han held the position of True Mother.

53 Sun Myung Moon, "Ideal Nation of God," February 21, 1980.

54 Ibid.

55 Author's personal testimony.

56 Elder, Timothy, Interview by author, Winter 2018.

57 Sun Myung Moon, "America and God's Will," September 18, 1976.

58 Ibid.

59 Sun Myung Moon, "Parents, Children and the World Centered Upon Oneself," June 5, 1983.

60 Hyung Jin Sean Moon, "Constitution of the United States of Cheon Il Guk," October 11, 2015, Preamble.

61 Sun Myung Moon, "The Coronation Ceremony of the Kingship of God," January 13, 2000.

62 "World Rally for Korean Freedom," https://www.youtube.com/watch?v=nzjuaZ9W3C8&t=2s

63 The fourth son of Reverend Sun Myung Moon.

64 A Saeilo engineer.

65 Saeilo is a business founded by Reverend Moon in 1981. It is a leading supplier of computer numerical control (CNC) machine tools and applications engineering.

66 The fifth son of Reverend Sun Myung Moon.

67 Unification Theological Seminary. Originally located in Barrytown, New York, UTS was founded by Reverend Moon in 1975,

68 Williams, J. Douglas, Interview by author, Spring 2019.

69 The Commander of the Lord's army is a Christophany (see chapter 1).

70 Chuck Baldwin, *To Keep or Not to Keep: Why Christians Should Not Give Up Their Guns* (Kalispell, Montana, 2013), p. 82.

71 Baldwin, *To Keep or Not to Keep*.

72 Ibid.

73 Sun Myung Moon, "Part 37 Organization and Outreach in Chaotic

Times," *Sun Myung Moon's Life In His Own Words,* https://www.tparents.org/Moon-Books/SunMyungMoon-Life/SunMyung-Moon-Life-37.htm

74 Sun Myung Moon, "The Age of Judgment and Ourselves," November 21, 1976.

75 *The Sermons of the Reverend Sun Myung Moon,* Vol. 448, p.241, May 9, 2004.

76 *The Sermons of the Reverend Sun Myung Moon,* Vol. 603, p.322, November 27, 2008.

77 Sun Myung Moon, "Parents, Children and the World Centered Upon Oneself," June 5, 1983.

78 Sun Myung Moon placed a crown (previously worn by himself) on the head of his son Hyung Jin Sean Moon on January 15, 2009, in Korea, January 31, 2009 in Korea, and January 31, 2009 in the United States (possible because of the time difference).

79 Hyung Jin Sean Moon, "The Constitution of the United States of Cheon Il Guk." October 11, 2015, p.3.

80 A & E (Arts & Entertainment) is an American television network which focuses primarily on non-fiction programming.

81 "A & E Documentary Cults and Extreme Belief Exposed, Unedited, Uncut," https://www.youtube.com/watch?v=oHgMlH0EciI

82 Ibid

83 Sun Myung Moon, "Inauguration Ceremony for the Peace Kingdom Corps and the Peace Kingdom Police," June 12, 2006.

84 These words are part of True Father's prayer given at Hyung Jin Sean Moon's Inauguration Ceremony as the World President in 2008.

Made in the USA
Middletown, DE
07 February 2020